# TECHNOLOGY, EDUCATION—CONNECTIONS
## THE TEC SERIES

*Series Editor:* Marcia C. Linn
*Advisory Board:* Robert Bjork, Chris Dede, Joseph Krajcik, Carol Lee,
Jim Minstrell, Jonathan Osborne, Mitch Resnick, Constance Steinkuehler

Data Literacy for Educators: Making It Count in
Teacher Preparation and Practice
ELLEN MANDINACH AND EDITH S. GUMMER

Assessing the Educational Data Movement
PHILIP J. PIETY

The New Science Education Leadership:
An IT-Based Learning Ecology Model
JANE F. SCHIELACK AND STEPHANIE L. KNIGHT, EDITORS

Digital Teaching Platforms:
Customizing Classroom Learning for Each Student
CHRIS DEDE AND JOHN RICHARDS, EDITORS

Leading Technology-Rich Schools:
Award-Winning Models for Success
BARBARA B. LEVIN AND LYNNE SCHRUM

The Learning Edge: What Technology Can Do to
Educate All Children
ALAN BAIN AND MARK E. WESTON

Learning in the Cloud:
How (and Why) to Transform Schools with
Digital Media
MARK WARSCHAUER

Video Games and Learning: Teaching and
Participatory Culture in the Digital Age
KURT SQUIRE

Teaching and Learning in Public:
Professional Development Through Shared Inquiry
STEPHANIE SISK-HILTON

Rethinking Education in the Age of Technology:
The Digital Revolution and Schooling in America
ALLAN COLLINS AND RICHARD HALVERSON

The Computer Clubhouse: Constructionism and
Creativity in Youth Communities
YASMIN B. KAFAI, KYLIE A. PEPPLER,
AND ROBBIN N. CHAPMAN, EDITORS

WISE Science:
Web-Based Inquiry in the Classroom
JAMES D. SLOTTA AND MARCIA C. LINN

Creating and Sustaining Online Professional
Learning Communities
JONI K. FALK AND BRIAN DRAYTON, EDITORS

Designing Coherent Science Education:
Implications for Curriculum, Instruction, and Policy
YAEL KALI, MARCIA C. LINN, AND JO ELLEN ROSEMAN,
EDITORS

Data-Driven School Improvement:
Linking Data and Learning
ELLEN B. MANDINACH AND MARGARET HONEY, EDITORS

Electric Worlds in the Classroom: Teaching and
Learning with Role-Based Computer Games
BRIAN M. SLATOR AND ASSOCIATES

Meaningful Learning Using Technology:
What Educators Need to Know and Do
ELIZABETH A. ASHBURN AND ROBERT E. FLODEN, EDITORS

Using Technology Wisely:
The Keys to Success in Schools
HAROLD WENGLINSKY

D1507400

# Data Literacy for Educators

## Making It Count in Teacher Preparation and Practice

Ellen B. Mandinach
Edith S. Gummer

Foreword by Barbara Schneider

**TEACHERS COLLEGE PRESS**

**TEACHERS COLLEGE** | COLUMBIA UNIVERSITY

NEW YORK AND LONDON

WestEd.org

Published simultaneously by Teachers College Press, 1234 Amsterdam Avenue, New York, NY 10027, and WestEd, 730 Harrison Street, San Francisco, CA 94107.

Cover design by David K. Kessler. Cover photo by Getty Images.

*Library of Congress Cataloging-in-Publication Data*

Names: Mandinach, Ellen Beth, author. | Gummer, Edith S., author.
Title: Data literacy for teachers : making it count in teacher preparation
    and practice / Ellen B. Mandinach, Edith S. Gummer ; foreword by Barbara
    Schneider.
Description: New York, NY : Teachers College Press, 2016. | Series:
    Technology, education-connections | Includes bibliographical references
    and index.
Identifiers: LCCN 2015047580| ISBN 9780807757543 (hardcover) | ISBN
    9780807757536 (pbk.) | ISBN 9780807774694 (ebook)
Subjects: LCSH: Education—Data processing. | Education—Decision making. |
    Information literacy. | Teachers—In-service training.
Classification: LCC LB1028.43 .M3619 2016 | DDC 370.71/1—dc23
LC record available at http://lccn.loc.gov/2015047580

ISBN 978-0-8077-5753-6 (paper)
ISBN 978-0-8077-5754-3 (hardcover)
ISBN 978-0-8077-7469-4 (ebook)

Printed on acid-free paper
Manufactured in the United States of America

23  22  21  20  19  18  17  16          8  7  6  5  4  3  2  1

*Ellen dedicates this book to the two men in her life, Eli and Houdi, without whom life would be so much less interesting and meaningful. You make every day better with your presence, love, support, and your humor. Both of you have taught me a great deal about using data to inform my decision making.*

*Edith dedicates this book to her two sons, who are engineers, and their families. Charles and Max know the importance of data and have weathered the emphasis on evidence all of the time they were growing up.*

# Contents

Foreword   Barbara Schneider        ix

Acknowledgments        xi

**1. Introduction to Data Literacy**        **1**

The Use of Data in Other Disciplines        2

The Use of Data in Education        3

Tools to Support Data-Driven Decision Making        4

The Roots of Data Use: What Research Says        4

Background Information for This Book        14

The Structure of the Book        16

The Audience for the Book        17

**2. The Context for Data Literacy**        **19**

The Policy Landscape        19

The Conflation of Data Literacy and Assessment Literacy:
The Importance of the Distinction        34

**3. The Conceptual Framework for Data Literacy for Teachers**        **38**

How We Determined the Knowledge and Skills
Needed for Data Literacy For Teachers        39

The Components and Elements of Data Literacy for Teachers        47

Open Invitation for Dialogue on Data Use for Teaching        55

**4. Beyond Knowledge and Skills:
Examining Values, Beliefs, and Dispositions Toward Data Use**        **57**

Research Findings on Teachers' Beliefs About Data Use        58

Beliefs and Dispositions: Essential Supports for Data Literacy for Teachers    59

5.  **Improving Data Literacy Among Educators:**
    **A Study of Four Schools of Education**                                   **65**

An Overview of the Schools of Education                                        65

How the Schools Integrate the Use of Data in Their Curricula                   66

Generalizability of the Data-Related Program Components                        76

Implications for Schools of Education                                          81

6.  **Data Literacy in Schools of Education: The Current Landscape**          **84**

A Representative Survey of Data Literacy in Schools of Education               84

The Process of Developing a Teacher Focus on Data                             88

Emerging Trends in Educating for Data Literacy                                92

7.  **Establishing Data Literacy for Teachers:  A Systemic Approach**         **94**

Taking a Systems Approach Toward Building Data Literacy in Educators           94

Key Stakeholder Groups in Improving Data Literacy for Teachers                95

What Changes Are Needed to Increase
    the Capacity for Effective Data Literacy                                  103

8.  **Helping Schools of Education Adopt Data Literacy for Teachers**        **109**

The Pedagogical Implications of Data Use                                      109

What Data Literacy Looks Like                                                 110

Charting a Pathway Toward Action                                              115

Conclusion                                                                    128

**References**                                                               **133**

**Index**                                                                    **147**

**About the Authors**                                                        **159**

# Foreword

We live in a time of accessible digitized knowledge that is constantly evolving as new scientific understandings have immersed our daily lives. Unlike earlier generations where change happened slowly, ours is occurring within a decade or days. There are hundreds of thousands of classroom teachers whose lives have witnessed major technological transformations. In most schools there are teachers who nostalgically remember learning the keyboard on a typewriter, pressing buttons on a stationary phone to place a call, or searching for curricular units and practices in paper card catalogues found in libraries of print books, journals, and pamphlets.

Today's teachers are being asked to keep up with a constantly expanding realm of data boxed in statistical evidence wrapped with new facts, figures, and projections. Pluto, that once far off last planet in our solar system was dropped in 2005 from the list of planets only to resurface as a dwarf planet. We passed the million-word threshold in the English dictionary in 2009, incorporating new phrases such as carbon footprint. Black rhinos became extinct in 2011 and scientists claim that there are millions more species of animals and plants yet to be found and catalogued. The Higgs boson or Higgs particle sometimes referred to as "God's particle" joined the list of force particles in 2012, ushering in new discoveries about our universe. Computer chips in 2014 began development to mimic human brains and robots have been shown to work together without human supervision.

In 2015, there were more than 7.2 billion living people throughout the globe. How many people will there be 5 years from now? What will it take to feed, clothe, and house them all? What jobs will they have? How and where will they travel? What diseases may they contract or recover from? If you wanted to know the answers to these questions, where would you look, what information would you need to estimate the answers, and how accurate would you be?

Big core ideas, driving purposeful questions, engaging students in science or any other subject, have significantly altered what teachers need to know to access data and what to do with it to enhance learning and become role models for their students. This thoughtful, well-organized book raises the challenges that beginning and experienced teachers face in becoming more data literate to increase their pedagogical effectiveness in their classrooms. The book is not just about data, trying to gain a fix on our knowledge explosion is a humongous task unto itself. What the authors comprehensively examine are the skills and knowledge teachers need to use data effectively and responsibly.

Coining the term *data literacy for teachers* (DLFT), the authors begin by demonstrating how societal values and individual predilections are impacting teachers' sensitivity and responsiveness to the emerging data demand of school systems. Not all schools have data cultures that embrace collaborative inquiry and the leadership to support its use by the principal and other leaders among the staff, and integrated technology systems. With such an organization in place it is possible to alter and modify teachers' as well as other school personnel's perceptions and use of multiple data sources for learning and practice. These conclusions are steeped in a thorough examination of recent studies and reports by various policy groups.

The definition of DLFT is unique, compelling, and, most importantly, specific in addressing how the construct intersects with data use in teaching taking into account adult learning theory and the situational context where teachers work. Why this definition is especially persuasive are four case studies that articulate how schools of education are improving teachers' data literacy. Here are real life examples of how to integrate data literacy into the teacher education program that are also discussed as applicable for professional development of experienced teachers and other school staff. While the synthesis of what works is convincing, the authors also point out what we do not know what might constrain teachers from adopting, sustaining, and improving their data literacy. There remain important topics yet to be researched.

While there are still some ambiguities with respect to broad-scale preparation for data literacy, the authors conclude with a detailed roadmap of what needs to happen today, right now, as the pressures and demand on teachers to be data-literate are critical. One key aspect of the authors' timely call for action is a cautionary discussion of not only what data can and cannot tell us, but why and how issues of confidentiality and generalizability regarding all types of information must be central to the formation of date literacy. We talk about the value of numeracy and literacy, but there is something incomparable about data literacy that we are only beginning to appreciate especially for the work lives of teachers, their students, and, for that matter, all of us.

—*Barbara Schneider*

# Acknowledgments

Many contributions of various types contributed to our work and made this book possible. Contributors included the organizations for which we work, colleagues, collaborators, and funding agencies. Our thinking has emerged through a collaborative process and has been informed by the work of many others in the field who have a created a tight-knit and sharing group of scholars. We are grateful for the support and insights we have received.

First and foremost, we would like to acknowledge WestEd for its organizational support of the work around data-driven decision making. Its creation of the Data for Decisions Initiative (DDI) has been essential to our work and has helped establish the importance of data-driven decision making within the agency and beyond with the creation of the AERA SIG on Data Use. We give special thanks to Sri Ananda, who has been a true supporter of our work, for spearheading the initiative within WestEd; and to Glen Harvey for her willingness to take a risk on the DDI. The DDI was a joint inspiration helped by the insights and support of Marty Orland. Marty challenged Ellen to make a go of the data work and that was the foundation for the DDI. His support has been unwavering.

Thanks also go out to Max McConkey, Danny Torres, and Christian Holden: to Max, whose creativity helped brand the DDI by considering a few names whose acronyms would not have worked in education; to Danny for his help on the book contract; and to Christian for his help on the graphics. Also thanks to the members of WestEd's IS Department who helped design the DDI website.

And thanks to two colleagues who have worked extremely hard on various projects for the DDI: first, Cathy Trapani, who joined WestEd as a psychometrician, for helping us on the assessments of data literacy for teachers; and second, Jeremy Friedman, whose work on these projects was invaluable. Jeremy's intelligence, dedication, sense of humor, and ability to put up with us helped make the work pleasurable. We miss your presence at WestEd.

Thanks are also due to colleagues in the Division of Research on Learning in the Directorate for Education and Human Resources at the National Science Foundation, and to the Research and Policy program at the Ewing

Marion Kauffman Foundation. Both organizations have a continuing strong commitment to ensuring that data in education is meaningful and relevant.

We would like to acknowledge the contributions of some external collaborators and colleagues whose work in the area of data use has influenced our thinking. Diana Nunnaley, the director of Using Data Solutions, has been a constant presence in our work, as a partner in the DDI and as a voice of the practice perspective. We cannot thank her enough for grounding us in the real world of schools and classrooms and providing salient examples of practice. Jeff Wayman, with his collaboration and ever-present wit, has provided feedback and collegiality for over a decade. We also acknowledge other researchers, advisory board members, and friends in the field of data-driven decision making, in particular Laura Hamilton of RAND, Chris Padilla of SRI, Jere Confrey of North Carolina State University, Jo Beth Jimerson of Texas Christian University, and Elizabeth Farley-Ripple of the University of Delaware. We give a special thank you to Barbara Schneider of Michigan State University for writing the preface to this volume. Barbara has a broad view of education, having been a president of the American Educational Research Association and a dean of a school of education. She understands the importance of data use in education.

Ellen and the projects have benefited immensely from close collaboration with the Data Quality Campaign (DQC), in particular Brennan McMahon Parton, Paige Kowalski, and Aimee Guidera. It is a valued partnership.

We also would like to acknowledge our funders and program officers who have made this work a reality. The data work began with a small grant from the Spencer Foundation to explore what schools of education are doing about data literacy among educators. That work produced our article in the *Educational Researcher* (Mandinach & Gummer, 2013a) that brought national attention to the issues around data literacy. This was followed by two other Spencer grants: one to bring researchers together to explore what is needed for a research agenda around data-driven decision making; and the second to develop scenarios to measure data literacy for teachers. We thank Andrea Bueschel for believing in our work.

We thank the Bill and Melinda Gates Foundation for the initial grant that launched the data literacy work. This funding allowed us to develop an in-depth understanding of the landscape around the resources and professional development that support data use in education. Most importantly, the project allowed us to bring together an amazingly thoughtful group to discuss how experts view data literacy.

We thank the Michael and Susan Dell Foundation for funding the landscape project. Micah Sagebiel provided insightful help as a program officer and as a participant in the case studies. Micah has been a real supporter of our work. Also Ashley Craddock, as a professional writer, took prose that was too "researchy" and made it approachable to more general audiences for the case studies and the MSDF blogs.

Finally, thanks to CAEP (the Council for the Accreditation of Educator Preparation) for the opportunity to conduct the workshops on data use, targeted to deans of schools of education. CAEP gave us the chance to get in front of the administrators of schools of education to help them understand the importance of data literacy. We can only hope that some of the attendees have taken our message to heart and begun to consider how to integrate data literacy into their teacher preparation programs.

A last set of acknowledgements pertains to the titling of this book. First, we acknowledge Ellen's husband, Eli Gruber, who thought the book should be entitled *Fifty Shades of Data* so perhaps it would sell. Second, after Ruth Neild, the Commissioner of the Institute of Education Sciences, gave an impassioned speech to the STATS-DC data conference in 2013 describing her love for data inquiry, we were tempted to use the title *Confessions of a Data Nerd*.

—*Ellen B. Mandinach*
*Edith S. Gummer*

# CHAPTER 1

# Introduction to Data Literacy

Data-driven decision making is not new in education. Good teachers and administrators have been collecting and using data for a very long time. In classrooms teachers observe how students react, behave, or perform. They assess whether students are engaged, attentive, and alert. They determine if students understand materials covered in class. They identify learning strengths and weaknesses. And then they make decisions about what instructional steps, social and emotional supports, and accommodations are indicated for students to progress. A teacher might discover that a student's reading difficulties are based on a vision problem rather than a cognitive issue. A teacher might find out that a student is being bullied and that is impacting the ability to focus on classroom activities. A teacher might learn that a student's home conditions make it impossible to complete homework assignments. These are examples of how various sources of data can inform how teachers interact with students and seek remedial steps for cognitive, motivational, and other issues.

Administrators also rely extensively on data. Data are used to make personnel, hiring, and tenure decisions. Data are used to make curricular and programmatic decisions. They are used to make financial decisions, disciplinary decisions, and transportation decisions, as well as decisions in many other areas of education management. Data can help administrations make a decision about whether there is a need for new curriculum materials. Data can inform administrators about whether it is cost-effective to add classroom aides in a school. Data can inform administrators about the impact of transportation schedules on behavior patterns or student performance.

How important has data literacy become? In some school districts, data literacy has become an essential skill set. As part of the application process, candidates for school building leaders must demonstrate their ability to use data from simulated data sets to design school improvement plans. The ability to use data now impacts hiring decisions for teachers in some districts.

These are examples of decision making in education. A question, however, emanates from the examples. How do districts make such hiring decisions if it is unclear what data literacy is and what skills and knowledge are needed? The intent is good, but how do the districts distinguish good data use from less effective data use? Are there instruments with predictive validity? Is it a matter of, when they see good or poor data use, they recognize it? Our effort to define what it means to be data literate and to outline specific skills and knowledge attempts to address these issues.

Data use has become essential in education. Pretty much every decision in education can and should be based on hard evidence. But that is not always the case. Educators sometimes rely on anecdotes, personal experience, and snapshots of behavior that may not be considered objective, accurate, or complete. Because of increasing pressure to improve the rigor of education as a profession, there has been a growing emphasis on educators' practice to become data-driven, data-based, or data-informed over the past 15 years.

## THE USE OF DATA IN OTHER DISCIPLINES

### Medicine and Business

Education has taken its cues from other disciplines, for example, medicine and business. Doctors now walk into examination rooms with digital tablets that are linked to patient histories and powerful databases to aid in diagnoses. Of course, just as in education, experience plays an important role. However, evidence from medical tests and face-to-face observations meld with results from clinical trials and research reports to inform the decision-making process. Medical professionals use such data for informed diagnoses that lead to decisions for appropriate courses of treatment. These decisions may be immediate or longer term, depending on the context. Good doctors have been making data-driven decisions for decades.

Businesses have some of the most sophisticated and comprehensive data systems that track inventory, purchasing histories, and pricing structures. Such systems provide information on what is or is not selling, how much has been sold, and projections for restocking. They can even determine how customers walk through stores to make purchases or where to place specific items to maximize attention that may lead to sales. Online sales rely on data systems that maintain data over time on customers' prior purchases, using the information to produce suggestions for future sales. Such emerging data systems have been developed to provide invaluable information to company officials and store managers, but the fundamental use of the data is not new. Before the technology, store owners took periodic and annual inventory from which decisions could be made about merchandising. They accumulated hand-written records of sales and examined shelf space before computing power was available.

## Sports

Even sports have become data driven. The book *Moneyball* is a prime example of using data to make decisions at all levels of the baseball operation (Lewis, 2004). Other sports have also jumped on the data analytics bandwagon, particularly basketball and football. Recently an article titled "Considered a Data Dinosaur, Tennis Is Trying an Analytic Approach" appeared in the *New York Times* (Robson, 2015). The article describes how tennis coaches and players are beginning to analyze data about matches and trends in and across points to enhance player performance. Coaches are coming to matches armed with iPads with data analytics apps that can identify strengths and weaknesses of their players and their opponents. The data then can be used to provide performance feedback in the short term, such as in a match, or in the long term.

Coaches need to determine how to communicate the results to maximize impact. This kind of communication is also essential in classroom instructional data use. That means figuring out what the right information is and what it means. The article notes that tennis has been a dinosaur, a sport resistant to use statistics. In part this is because longitudinal data may be problematic to interpret because of players' trajectories of performance and ratings. It also may be because the data cannot address specific performance-related issues, such as failing to follow through on a shot, overrunning the ball, or tossing the ball in the wrong place. The data can help discern trends that can inform match strategies and tactics. In the case of classroom instruction, the data can also reinforce and confirm observations, informal data, and even gut feelings. According to Robson (2015),

> Armed with new information, tennis coaches now have a more efficient way to gather, arrange, and disseminate critical metrics for on-court visits. They can also log into a database with thousands of matches on every player, which can facilitate practice sessions and scouting reports. (p. B8)

## THE USE OF DATA IN EDUCATION

So is data-driven decision making new? Absolutely not. It has been around for a long time, particularly in other professions. However, the emphasis or importance of data use in education is increasing now, and for good reason. Educators are being confronted with more and diverse data than ever before. Data sources have proliferated. We name just a few sources here:

- Assessments: summative, formative, interim, benchmark, diagnostic
- Classroom activities: exercises, quizzes, reports, problem sets, lab exercises, projects, demonstrations

- Portfolios
- Observations: attentiveness, engagement, fatigue, hyperactivity, hunger, misbehavior
- Questions and answers
- Attendance, truancy, and tardiness
- Behavior: demerits, expulsions, socially supportive actions
- Health and nutrition
- Affect: motivation, attitude, attention, grit
- Special status: disabilities, special education status, accommodations, language, giftedness
- Transportation
- Demographics
- Home circumstances: parental status, parental education, number of siblings, homelessness, language barrier, immigration status, poverty level, parental support, home educational resources, technology

## TOOLS TO SUPPORT DATA-DRIVEN DECISION MAKING

The myriad of data is quite mind-boggling and its diversity is certainly more than human memory capacity can handle. Consequently, one major and emerging trend is the increasing availability of technological tools to support the use of data. These tools range from huge data systems to mobile devices to simple spreadsheets. They include data warehouses, student information systems, instructional management systems, assessment systems, diagnostic devices, data dashboards, electronic grade books, spreadsheets, and much more. The technologies help educators access, store, and examine data. They can help manage instruction, develop assessments, create graphical representations of results, and produce reports. Some facilitate data interpretation. But to be clear, the tools should be used to provide assistance, not to replace the judgment of the educators. Teachers still need to interpret the data or results in light of the course content and then determine what instructional steps are appropriate. This is what we have termed data literacy for teachers (DLFT), a construct that is the focus of this book and is dealt with in depth in later chapters. Data literacy for teachers is an amalgam of skills, knowledge, and dispositions that teachers need to be able to use data effectively and responsibly.

## THE ROOTS OF DATA USE: WHAT RESEARCH SAYS

Because data-driven decision making and data literacy reside within the context of a complex system, it is important for us to provide an overview of salient research that informs data use in classrooms, schools, and districts.

Enculturating data use requires many necessary components, supports, and resources (Hamilton, Halverson, Jackson, Mandinach, Supovitz, & Wayman, 2009), such as strong leadership, a vision for data use, data teams and data coaches, appropriate technology, and educators who know how to use data. We briefly describe the components and how they relate to the need for data literacy.

## Implementation Components

As is noted in the review of research found in the Institute of Education Sciences (IES) Practice Guide titled *Using Student Achievement Data to Support Instructional Decision Making* (Hamilton et al., 2009), the major components of effective data use are the following: establishment of a data culture, an explicit vision for data use, strong leadership, provision of data teams and data coaches, and technology to support data use.

*A Data Culture.* It is essential for schools and districts to create a data culture in which data use is expected, supported, and sustained (Hamilton et al., 2009; Mandinach, 2012). Data cultures are typically built on the notion of collaborative inquiry (Love, Stiles, Mundry, & DiRanna, 2008) where educators identify problems of practice, collect and analyze data, implement a potential solution, determine impact, and iterate as needed (Easton, 2009, 2010; Hamilton et al., 2009; Mandinach, Honey, Light, & Brunner, 2008; Means, Padilla, & Gallagher, 2010). Data cultures have strong leadership and resources in which educators can explore, examine, and discuss data within a trusting environment.

Schools where leadership have given teachers the chance to have open and frank discussions about student performance tend to have a strong data culture. Teachers feel free to discuss where they may be struggling with particular students and seek advice from colleagues about potential strategies that might be implemented. The teachers do not fear that admitting a problem will negatively impact their evaluations or that colleagues will deem them ineffective.

Another example of enculturation is the provision for common meeting time around data work. Some school districts have set aside time to be used solely for data inquiry. For example, one large urban district has no classes that meet on Wednesday afternoons. They are called "Wednesday outs." Teachers meet in data teams to discuss student performance or receive additional training on data use. Setting aside such dedicated time makes a strong statement about the importance of data.

The cultures are guided by an explicit vision for why data are being collected and used to inform their work. Leadership expects educators to use data in their practice. The expectation resonates throughout the school from the principal's office to the data clerks. Leaders make it clear that the use of data is expected. They model the use of data. They use data. They communicate with data, not gut feelings. They are armed with data. Data become completely integrated into the practices of all educators.

Love and colleagues (2008) provide information about seven components they see as essential for the establishment of data cultures:

- Enculturate the notion of continuous improvement
- Build support from stakeholders
- Strengthen collaboration
- Empower a data coach
- Organize a data team
- Create time for collaboration
- Provide timely access to data (pp. 29–30)

Datnow and Park (2009) also outline a process for enculturating data within a school. Their structure is a six-step process:

1. Schools must lay a foundation for data-driven decision making.
2. There must be an emphasis on continuous improvement.
3. A school must incorporate the use of an information management system.
4. Educators must select the right data.
5. They need to build capacity.
6. The school needs to analyze and act on data to improve performance. (p. 195)

*A Vision for Data Use.* Staff in schools and districts need to understand why they are being asked or required to use data. Such a rationale can be found in the form of a vision statement that comes from leadership at all levels. Ideally, the vision is aligned between central and building leadership so the purposes for district and school data use are understood. It must be explicit so that educators understand its purpose, and it should be linked to and integrated with school improvement plans and educational objectives (Hamilton et al., 2009) and incorporated into a written plan. Having explicit norms and expectations are an important part of the vision (Wohlstetter, Datnow, & Park, 2008).

Showing how systemic and interconnected the components of data-driven decision making are, a vision for data can be communicated by establishing data cultures (Datnow, Park, & Wohlstetter, 2007; Rose, 2006), by creating collaborative data teams (Datnow et al., 2007; Feldman & Tung, 2001; Knapp, Swinnerton, Copland, & Monpas-Huber, 2006; Wayman, Cho, & Johnston, 2007), by developing a data plan (Armstrong & Anthes, 2001; Datnow et al., 2007; Mason, 2002), and by providing common planning time for data teams to meet.

*Leadership.* Having strong leadership to support data use is one of the most pervasive findings in research on data-driven decision making (Copland, Knapp, & Swinnerton, 2009; Datnow & Park, 2010, 2014; Lachat & Smith, 2005; Leithwood, Louis, Anderson, & Walhstrom, 2007). We cannot state strongly enough how important it is for leaders, particularly building leaders, to believe in data use. Principals set the stage in schools and give cues to staff about appropriate and expected behavior. It is important for principals to model data use, use evidence when speaking, set a vision that provides a rationale for data use, make clear that data are expected to be used, and provide the necessary resources to make possible data use within the school.

For example, teachers take their cues from leadership. Teachers see that their building leaders use data, modeling their commitment to the use of data when communicating to stakeholders, teachers, and parents. Teachers are expected to also use data when communicating with parents, students, and colleagues. Conversely, we have heard teachers ask why they should be using data when their principals do not use data but require them to do so.

Research and practice support the notion of distributed leadership around data (Copland et al., 2009, Lachat & Smith, 2005; Love et al., 2008). Distributed leadership allows for shared responsibility, rather than placing the burden on one individual. It is especially important given the mobility of educators; that is, if a leader leaves, there are other individuals who can sustain the data work. Distributed leadership also can help compensate for a principal who does not believe in data use.

Central leadership also is important. Having a superintendent who believes in and supports data use helps create a culture for data use, with expectations that data use is important. Just as with building leaders, superintendents can model data use through communication with educators, school board members, parents, and the general public. They can use concrete results when making presentations. They can seek out reports that are based on sound analytics. They can make it clear that decisions must be based on concrete evidence. Ideally, there needs to be an alignment between central and building leadership in terms of the messages they give about why data are being used.

*Data Coaches and Data Teams.* Establishing data teams and providing data coaches—teachers or administrators who are adept at using data and working well with colleagues—are some of the most important supports to make data use possible in a school. Love and colleagues (2008) provide concrete steps to data teaming and coaching, identifying five data coach activities. First, data coaches help *build* the foundation for data-driven decision making, focusing on determining and sensing the needs of the schools. The coach is essential in establishing the work of the data team. Second, data coaches help *identify* the problems or student learning issues to which data can be applied. Third, data coaches help colleagues verify the possible causes of the problems. Fourth, the data coaches facilitate the generation of possible solutions. Finally, data coaches work with colleagues to implement the solutions and monitor outcomes.

Data coaches, mentors, or facilitators take responsibility within a school for leading colleagues through the exploration of data. These individuals can be drawn from the ranks of teachers, administrators, or content experts. They can even be fellows who come from the Strategic Data Project at Harvard University (2015) and provide training for local and state educators, who then return to their education agencies as data experts. The data coaches help create data teams, facilitate data use, assist colleagues to collect, analyze, and interpret data, and provide training to other staff members.

There are a few caveats that pertain to data coaches. First, it is not necessary for them to be the proverbial statistics geeks. On the contrary, data coaches ideally should be adept at working with people and communicating about data. Also ideally, there should be multiple data coaches to avoid burnout, overburdening, or mobility issues (Hamilton et al., 2009). Distributing this responsibility helps create a stronger base of knowledge about data use than if it resides only in one individual.

Data teams are collaborative working groups, tasked with collecting, analyzing, and interpreting data. They can be structured in diverse ways. They might be departmentally based (e.g., all math teachers). They might be within a course (e.g., all the biology teachers). They might be a vertical team comprised of elementary-level teachers who cross grade levels to engage in longitudinal performance assessment of students as needed. Data teams also are tasked with helping increase the data literacy among other educators within a school, using a turnkey model.

Collaboration around data has clearly been shown to be an essential component in the implementation of data-driven practices throughout a school (Datnow & Park, 2010; Hamilton, et al., 2009; Long, Rivas, Light, & Mandinach, 2008; Wayman, 2005). Collaboration emphasizes the need for shared ideas, common terms, the interrogation of data, and discussion of outcomes among colleagues so that educators can learn from one another. Collaboration in a data teaming environment enables educators to discuss pressing educational issues and problems around student learning, performance, and behavior. It provides a venue in which teachers can share opinions about possible instructional insights and strategies to remediate student performance issues. It is essential that collaboration be based on mutual trust where colleagues can learn from one another and recognize that others may have a solution to a problem that one of them may lack. Part of the issue is teacher ego; another part is teacher trust; and a third issue is not fearing retribution for being open about needing help. It is helpful if teachers are open to input from others, leaving their egos at the door. Means and colleagues (2010) found that 90% of schools report that educators feel comfortable collaborating this way and 59% know how to work with colleagues. Mason (2002) noted that using data in classrooms is essential but it had not gone far enough. Teachers need time to learn from each other about instructional strategies to address particular problems. Thus the collaborative process in data teaming promotes shared responsibility for student learning.

Here is an example of the work of data coaches and data teams:[1]

Teachers in an elementary school in an urban district worked on data under the leadership of a passionate data coach. They convened in a data team that met routinely, but also had special "data days" following major assessment and instructional events. The principal ensured the provision for these data meetings, protecting the time and noting the importance of the data work. The purposes of these meetings were to collaboratively examine results and consider the implications for instruction and practice more generally. The team analyzed different sources of data, hoping to identify and understand students' weaknesses and strengths based on the data in each data set. The triangulation among the diverse data sources helped the team reveal different aspects of performance, tell a story about the student, and uncover concerns the teachers need to address. Because the data team had a vertical structure (i.e., comprised of teachers across grade levels), the collaborative inquiry process facilitated teachers at all grade levels to examine longitudinal patterns as well as more current ones so that they could modify their instructional plans. The data coach facilitated the inquiry process and subsequent lesson planning. Teachers became more aware of students' learning needs through the examination of data and were able to collaboratively make strategic instructional adjustment to improve their classroom practices.

*Technology.* The technology to support data-driven decision making has changed significantly over the past decade. States have their statewide longitudinal data systems (SLDSs) that provide primarily accountability and compliance data from districts to the U.S. Department of Education (National Center for Education Statistics [NCES], 2015a). Many districts have data warehouses and student information systems that serve as repositories of their data (Means et al., 2010). Wayman (2005, 2007) subsequently outlined four major technology solutions: data warehouses, student information systems, instructional management systems, and assessment systems. More recently, systems have become integrated, providing diverse solutions rather than necessitating different technologies. The smallest districts may not have these sophisticated systems, but use only spreadsheets.

At the classroom level, handheld devices were developed to provide diagnostic assessments (Hupert, Heinze, Gunn, & Stewart, 2008). These were personal digital assistants such as Palm Pilots on which tests such as diagnostic mathematics and literacy measures were loaded, tests administered, and data collected. Data were then transferred to computers to analyze individual, class, and school data. More recently, data dashboards are being developed that provide real-time data to teachers (Arizona Department of Education, 2015). Dashboards are user interfaces that provide readily accessible, well-organized, and user-friendly data. Dashboards are also being developed to assist decision making for parents (Ewing Marion Kauffman Foundation, 2015). Dashboards are being used as early warning systems, for teacher observations, and other sorts of data collections. Assessment systems have become increasingly sophisticated, providing teachers with real-time data of student and class performance and linking them to state standards. The assessments are formative in nature rather than high-stakes, summative tests. Teachers can see student responses as they occur and can gain an understanding of student strengths and weaknesses that immediately inform subsequent instructional planning (Bergan, Burnham, Bergan, Callahan, & Feld, 2013).

Blended or personalized learning environments provide a host of technologies that enable creative teaching and learning activities and support data collection (Baker, 2014; Bienkowski, 2014; DiCerbo & Behrens, 2014; Dieterle, 2014). The technologies may include interactive whiteboards and mobile devices (e.g., cell phones and tablets).

Whiteboards allow teachers to project documents from their computers and collect student responses based on what has been written on the board. On mobile devices, students can submit assignments and assessments from anywhere at any time, doing the work at their own pace. Teachers can monitor student performance remotely.

### Learning How to Use Data

The assumption for most data use is that the ability to use data effectively or demonstrating data literacy is thought to change teacher practice (Chen, Heritage, & Lee, 2005; Kerr, Marsh, Ikemoto, Darilek, & Barney, 2006) and these changed practices then lead to improvement in achievement or student performance (Feldman & Tung, 2001; Schmoker & Wilson, 1995). Recognition by researchers and other stakeholders of the importance of data use has been sustained over time. Mitchell, Lee, and Herman (2000) note:

> Data-based decision making and use of data for continuous improvement are the operating concepts of the day. These new expectations, that schools monitor their efforts to enable all students to achieve, assume that school leaders and teachers are ready and able to use data to understand where students are academically and why, and to establish improvement plans that are targeted, responsive, and flexible. (p. 22)

Yet knowing how to use data is fundamental to the data-use process. As researchers have noted (Mandinach, 2012; Means et al., 2010; Wayman & Stringfield, 2006), few educators have taken courses on how to use data, and many are not prepared to use data effectively and do not exhibit data literacy. Data literacy, generically defined,—that is, the ability of instructional leaders and teachers to work individually and collectively to examine outcomes, trends, performance, and other indicators based on achievement data, formative assessment measures of student performance, students' work products, and other forms of data (e.g., demographic, affective, process, attitudes, behavioral), and to develop strategies for improvement based on these data—is now widely recognized as a critical strategy in the academic performance of schools (Duncan, 2009b; Easton, 2009; Fullan, 2000; Haycock, 2001; Johnson, 1996; Love, 2004; Schmoker, 1999; Zalles, 2005). The National Research Council (1996) noted over two decades ago that "far too often, more educational data are collected and analyzed than are used to make decisions or take action" (p. 90). Thus data must be actionable and have utility for educators to use them to inform practice (Mandinach & Gummer, 2012), and educators must know how to use the data.

Practitioners must be trained to use data, especially to understand how to translate data into actionable instructional practice (Herman & Gribbons, 2001; Mandinach & Honey, 2008; Mandinach, Honey, et al., 2008; Mason, 2002). The translation skills typically are not included in professional development (Mandinach & Gummer, 2011, 2013a). Without training in data-driven processes, such as how to use data, act on multiple sources of data, and transform data into actionable knowledge, too many educators draw only the most superficial conclusions from the data available, missing a wealth of opportunities to learn about the strengths and weaknesses of their educational practices. In the absence of systematic training in data literacy, principals tend to be trained before teachers. This turnkey model, with the first trained individual training colleagues, does not go far enough for broad data literacy. Further, educators at different levels of a school system have role-based, and often intuitive, approaches to the process (Mandinach & Honey, 2008; Marsh, Pane, & Hamilton, 2006) and may require different kinds of training. School administrators, for example, use high-stakes test data to understand *general* patterns of performance, identifying class-, grade-, and school-wide strengths and weaknesses so that they can allocate resources and plan professional development and other kinds of targeted intervention activities (e.g., after school remediation, summer school, and so on). Teachers tend to use multiple sources of data, such as homework assignments, in-class tests, and classroom performance, as well as impressionistic, anecdotal, and experiential information to shape their thinking about their students' strengths and weaknesses (Brunner et al., 2005; Honey et al., 2002; Light, Wexler, & Heinze, 2004; Mandinach,

Rivas, Light, & Heinze, 2006). Thus data literacy may be exhibited differently based on educators' roles within the system. For teachers, however, we believe that training on data skills must be integrated with their domain and pedagogical knowledge, a perspective which schools of education are uniquely positioned to address.

Data literacy also includes learning how to use data responsibly and ethically (DQC, 2015a; Mandinach, Parton, Gummer, & Anderson, 2015). Because of the growing skepticism about protecting data privacy and confidentiality in all domains, not just education, there is increasing pressure among educators to understand the ethics of data use and demonstrate the skills in their practice. *Phi Delta Kappan* ("Privacy and school data," 2015) devoted an entire issue to privacy to try and communicate its importance to practicing teachers. Yet, to our knowledge, no agencies, organizations, or institutions are taking responsibility for promoting the training of educators or communicating the necessary skills and knowledge to the education community, and it is unclear whose responsibility it is. The National Forum on Education Statistics (2010) released a guide to data ethics and offers an online course, but there is no comprehensive program for helping local educators understand the basics of data protection.

Despite encouragement at the policy level, there is growing consensus that educators and schools still are not adequately prepared to use data and create a culture of data use (Herman & Gribbons, 2001; Mandinach & Honey, 2008; Olsen, 2003). If schools are going to rise to the challenge of helping all students meet academic standards, then providing high-quality training for educators in how to use data to improve student performance is essential (Jennings, 2002; Mandinach, Rivas, et al., 2006; Schafer & Lissitz, 1987; Wise, Lukin, & Roos, 1991). The training must also extend to teacher preparation programs (Cibulka, 2013; Duncan, 2012a; Mandinach & Gummer, 2013a). The intent is to create a generation of educators who are data literate and demonstrate that literacy in their practice.

## Study Findings on Data-Driven Decision Making

There is substantial research about the importance of using data, but the amount of supporting research on effective data practice and impact is still lacking. The review of research on effective data use in the IES Practice Guide (Hamilton et al., 2009) found few studies on professional development programs intended to improve data use and few rigorous studies on data use and their impact. Some studies have recently begun to emerge. The IES-funded Center for Data-Driven Reform in Education (2011) focuses on district-level data-driven school reform. A study of this model provides initial results with positive student outcomes resulting from data use (Carlson, Borman, & Robinson, 2011), but the study does not deal with teachers' data skills. Research by Konstantopoulos, Miller, and van der Ploeg (2013) found data use improves student performance for some subjects and some grades. The focus here was on teachers within classrooms, but, again, the study did not address data literacy. A large study currently being conducted and funded by IES does include a professional development component, but the data skill set embedded in the training is not well articulated. In another Department of Education study, a national survey provided evidence of a continuing and pressing need for professional development on data use (Means et al., 2010). A follow-up study (Means, Chen, DeBarger, & Padilla, 2011) found that many teachers lack essential skills to use data effectively. Teachers do not routinely think critically about the relationships between instructional practices and student outcomes (Confrey & Makar, 2005; Hammerman & Rubin, 2002; Kearns & Harvey, 2000).

Data literacy is not just about individual educators, but also educators working in data teams, what is referred to as "collaborative inquiry." Means and colleagues (2011) examined individual teacher data literacy as well as group data literacy and found that groups can compensate for individuals' lack of knowledge and skills. Groups were more adept at seeking clarifications, identifying errors in information and computations, considering alternative explanations, following up on questions, and using background information. Groups also exhibited more correct responses than did individual teachers, as well as more engagement in working with data. In general, groups used a wider array of skills to inform decisions than did individuals. Data teaming plays an important role in the use of data, but individual skills and knowledge are also important.

Results from these Department of Education studies have yielded mixed results about the impact of data-driven decision making on student performance but do provide insights into the needed components of data use and the importance of data to inform practice. None of these studies, however, has focused specifically on laying out the landscape of the necessary skills and knowledge that teachers need to be data literate.

Here is an example of the power of data teaming:

An elementary school has weekly meetings in which teachers across grade levels discuss particularly problematic students and strategies to help these students improve. A 3rd-grade teacher admits to having difficulty reaching one student. She describes the steps she has taken to teach this student, but nothing has worked to date. The student's 2nd-grade teacher then shares some strategies that worked for her the previous year. The teachers jointly lay out a course of action that the 3rd-grade teacher can implement and then report back to the team about the outcomes.

## BACKGROUND INFORMATION FOR THIS BOOK

### Definitions

Before moving into the main part of this book, we provide here a few definitions for terms that undergird our thesis: *data, data-driven decision making,* and *data literacy for teachers.*

What are *data?* (Note that we refer to *data* as plural.) We see data as part of a continuum that moves from raw pieces of information ultimately to actionable knowledge that leads to a decision (Mandinach, Honey, et al., 2008). Data comprise quantitative or qualitative facts, figures, materials, or results. They are empirical pieces of evidence. They are transformed into information by context that gives them meaning. Information provides to the user the evidence for transformation to knowledge upon which decisions can be made and actions taken. The goal is for the data to be actionable, that is, to provide the needed information on which instruction or some other action can be taken.

*Data-driven decision making* at the simplest level is the use of data or evidence to inform a decision. A more comprehensive definition is provided in the IES Practice Guide on using data to impact student achievement (Hamilton et al., 2009). The authors define *data-based decision making* as

> teachers, principals, and administrators systematically collecting and analyzing various types of data, including demographic, administrative, process, perceptual, and achievement data, to guide a range of decisions to help improve the success of students and schools. (p. 46)

This is a generic perspective on data use in education.

Data literacy for teachers is a construct or concept we have developed in our research on data-driven decision making. It is a more targeted construct. We began working to understand what it means for teachers to be data literate, that is, to use data effectively and appropriately. We (Gummer & Mandinach, 2015; Mandinach, Friedman, & Gummer, 2015) define the construct as:

> Data literacy for teaching is the ability to transform information into actionable instructional knowledge and practices by collecting, analyzing, and interpreting all types of data (assessment, school climate, behavioral, snapshot, longitudinal, moment-to-moment, etc.) to help determine instructional steps. It combines an understanding of data with standards, disciplinary knowledge and practices, curricular knowledge, pedagogical content knowledge, and an understanding of how children learn.

## Foundations, Questions, and Goals

Our research consists of striving to identify and understand what skills, knowledge, and dispositions teachers use throughout the decision-making process. We differentiate between skills and knowledge, and dispositions. Our focus is primarily on the former although the latter are also important, since dispositions include beliefs and habits of mind about the use of data and using data responsibly. They include more generic activities such as collaboration, inquiry, and thinking critically. Our work also has entailed understanding how data skills interact with teachers' knowledge of their domain as well as their knowledge of pedagogy or pedagogical content knowledge (Shulman, 1986). As will be explicated in Chapter 3, we originally saw this as a three-way interaction with all three components influencing how decisions are made. As you will see in Chapter 3, we expand our conceptual framework even further.

Understanding the role of content knowledge and pedagogical content knowledge in decision making is a work in progress for us, with unanswered questions. For example, professionals other than educators need data skills. Statisticians, scientists, social scientists, researchers, and others are trained to use and interpret data within their disciplines. There will be essential disciplinary knowledge and skills applied to any problem of practice or situation. Some data skills (e.g., using technologies, accessing data, analyzing data) may be generic, but they must be customized within the context of the specific content area (e.g., how to adjust instruction based on data). This is why teachers need to combine their data skills with content knowledge and pedagogical content knowledge. The pedagogical component helps determine the instructional actions that result from the data embedded within the content area.

What we don't know is what the lowest acceptable levels of domain knowledge and pedagogical content knowledge are that will enable the effective transformation of data to information and ultimately to actionable instructional knowledge that leads to a decision. In a related manner, we also do not know when and where along the developmental continuum of teachers' careers (from preservice to experienced teacher) it is best to introduce data literacy skills, given the complex interplay of the ability to contextualize the data within the discipline. Introduce them too early and there may be confusion and ambiguity because teachers lack concrete experience and the necessary knowledge base. Introduce them too late and there is a missed opportunity to develop a critical skill set that is needed upon entering the classroom. Thus we have chosen to promote the idea that earlier is better than later. We also need to address whether it is better and more feasible to provide a stand-alone course on data-driven decision making or to integrate the concepts into existing courses in teacher preparation programs. We see the need for the stand-alone courses but feel strongly that the integrated approach better addresses the complex interactions with domain knowledge and pedagogy in teacher preparation programs.

This book reflects a huge amount of work and a heavy intellectual lift to develop a new construct and a definition, then have data literacy for teachers gain traction among researchers, policymakers, and practitioners. There is still more work to be accomplished. As we note from our own research and that of others, data literacy is still lacking among the current cohort of educators and in teacher preparation programs. We need better measures of the construct, ones that can be used by professors, professional development providers, school districts, researchers, and others. We need materials for courses, either for integration into existing courses or stand-alone courses in schools of education. We need the education landscape to recognize that there is a difference between data literacy and assessment literacy, and that the difference is real and important. We also need answers to some looming research questions around data literacy like those mentioned above.

We hope this book will resonate with the education community— schools of education, schools and school districts, policymakers, practitioners, and researchers. We have learned so much from practitioners as they struggle to make use of data. We hope this book gives back in some small way. We also hope that this book serves as a call to action for schools of education and policymakers to help develop the next generation of educators who are data literate.

## THE STRUCTURE OF THE BOOK

Chapter 2 provides the foundation for data literacy. It furnishes the context for data literacy by outlining the current policy landscape that is emphasizing data use by educators, and draws on remarks by top policymakers and leaders of professional organizations to suggest why people think data use is important. The chapter examines relevant policy documents, standards, and requirements that pertain to both teacher preparation and data literacy in the context of teacher preparation and teacher practice. This chapter also explores some of the controversies surrounding data use, including the fear of overreaching, inappropriate, or intrusive data collection and violations of privacy and confidentiality that go hand in hand with the criticisms surrounding overtesting.

Chapters 3 and 4 outline the conceptual framework we have developed for the construct "data literacy for teachers." Chapter 3 describes the interaction among three domains of the construct—data use for teachers, content knowledge, and pedagogical content knowledge, as well as other inputs outlined by Shulman (1987, 2015). It then explores the specific skills and knowledge we have identified through our research and the components into which they fall. Chapter 3 also provides a deep dive into the skills and knowledge, providing concrete definitions of them and outlining what effective and less effective application of the skills look like. Chapter 4 moves beyond skills and knowledge to describe the dispositions involved in data use, such as collaboration and communication. The chapter lays out why these dispositions are important to data literacy for teachers.

Chapter 5 provides selected case studies or scenarios that illustrate exemplary or emerging practices in the area of data literacy in teacher preparation programs. It includes the description of a school of education that has been transformed into a model of data use by faculty and students as well as information obtained from three residency programs. We draw on the experiences of these institutions to extract components that might be applicable to assist other schools of education as they begin to address the data literacy issue.

Chapter 6 describes the venues for helping educators become data literate. It begins by exploring the point along the developmental continuum where it might be best to introduce various aspects of data literacy and addresses how schools of education can include stand-alone courses or integrate the concepts into existing curricula. It describes models of professional development that are currently being used to train teachers. The chapter then explores emerging trends and innovative ways of preparing educators when there are limited formal courses or professional development opportunities.

Chapter 7 addresses the systemic nature of establishing data literacy in education and explores the many challenges. It considers the organizations that are key players in recognizing and requiring data literacy to be part of educators' practice, and outlines the roles and responsibilities of the organizations. The chapter explores potential key levers for change. It challenges schools of education to step up and include data literacy in their teacher preparation programs.

The final chapter is a call to action. It summarizes the content of the volume, noting the key levers for change and the challenges. It describes what data literacy looks like. It includes an exploration of the pedagogical implications for teachers who are data literate and those who remain data novices. It explores what knowledge the research community needs to acquire, what actions policymakers need to take, and what steps the teacher preparation community should take to enhance educators' data literacy. The chapter concludes with an action plan of recommendations for different stakeholder groups.

## THE AUDIENCE FOR THE BOOK

The intent of this volume is to reach a broad education audience to make educators aware of the importance of improving their capacity to use data. It is no longer just an ancillary construct; it is a necessary set of skills, knowledge, and dispositions. Administrators and professors in schools of education are a key audience. We hope the book communicates the importance of beginning to integrate data literacy for teachers into their curricula and provides a sense of what is involved in the implementation process as well as the content. It is a book that should resonate with school district administrators who might be interested in enhancing their staff capacity to use data. Professional development providers might benefit from gaining an in-depth analysis of the "data literacy for teachers" construct to inform their programs. Educators who want to understand what is meant by data literacy and what skills and knowledge are included are another audience. Finally, the book is intended to resonate with other researchers in the field where data literacy can inform their own work. It is our hope that the volume serves to inform the education community that evidence matters in practice. Decisions must be informed by data. It is no longer sufficient to rely solely on experience, anecdotes, and gut feelings. All educators must be armed with data. It is now a necessity.

## NOTE

1. We thank Diana Nunnaley, the Director of Using Data Solutions, for providing the basis for this example.

# CHAPTER 2

# The Context for Data Literacy

This chapter provides context to help understand why data literacy for teachers is important. We begin by describing the policy landscape, drawing upon comments made by key educational leaders. We then outline the views of various professional organizations, noting how standards, licensure, and tests are involved in the move toward building educators' capacity to use data. We also discuss some of the issues that surround data use, in particular those that focus on the overemphasis on testing. We conclude by recognizing an issue in the field that continues to plague the implementation of data literacy for teachers, namely the conflation of data literacy with assessment literacy.

## THE POLICY LANDSCAPE

### Commentaries from Policymakers

Policymakers have been discussing data use for a long time but the transformation of discourse to policy has taken longer. If we look back over the past two federal administrations (G. W. Bush and Obama), we can see a subtle shift in the messaging. Before the Obama administration, most data, particularly at the federal level, have been collected for compliance and accountability purposes. The Statewide Longitudinal Data System (SLDS) Grant Program (NCES, 2015a) was initiated with the awarding of its first grants in 2005 to support the development of large data repositories at the state level. The intent of the SLDSs is to provide a venue for states to collect longitudinal data from districts and schools that can be used to improve student learning. These data systems, however, collect mostly accountability and performance data from districts and then send them to the U.S. Department of Education through the ED*Facts* data highway, described as follows:

> ED*Facts* is a U.S. Department of Education (ED) initiative to collect, analyze, report on and promote the use of high-quality, kindergarten through grade 12 (K–12) performance data for use in education planning, policymaking, and management and budget decisionmaking to improve outcomes for students. (U.S. Department of Education, 2015, p. 1)

The data that reside in the SLDSs and travel the ED*Facts* data highway may be helpful for states and districts to make broad decisions, but they are not at the level of granularity to provide schools and classrooms with the kind of data that can directly inform instruction, that is, data for the continuous improvement of schools, classrooms, and students.

The policy landscape addresses data-driven decision making in several areas: (1) data for compliance and accountability; (2) data for continuous improvement; (3) data for research and evaluation; (4) data for policy decisions; and (5) data for informing classroom practices. And they are not mutually exclusive categories. For example, policy decisions may overlap with accountability and continuous improvement decisions. Research can inform them as well as policy.

It is our feeling that when the highest level of education officials in the country talk convincingly about the need for data-driven decision making, it makes a compelling argument for all educators to know how to use data effectively and responsibly, but needs to go further. This messaging has been translated into policy for some, but not all, aspects of data use, for example, the protection of data privacy and confidentiality through the Family Educational Rights and Privacy Act (FERPA).

To illustrate the policy landscape of thinking about data literacy, we reviewed speeches by the former Secretary of Education Arne Duncan, the former director of the Institute of Education Sciences John Easton, and the IES current director Ruth Neild, all members of the Obama administration who have had a lot to say about the importance of data use in education. The messaging is slowly being translated into action; for example, including data use in the policies around improving teacher preparation (Teacher Preparation Issues, 2014; U.S. Department of Education, 2014; White House, 2014). Below we paraphrase and quote from these speeches to document the need for data literacy. It is important to note that the emphasis on data use and evidence in education gained traction in the G. W. Bush administration. Data use crosses party lines and can no longer be considered a passing fad. However, there was a perceived philosophical shift away from data use for accountability and compliance to data use for continuous improvement. Because of this shift, it is important to consider what the high-level policymakers are saying about data-driven decision making. We focus first on the general context of data use and then on the need for teachers to use data.

Duncan (2010c) makes clear that he sees data as a tool to change policy, guide reform, and inform instruction and student achievement. He speaks of unleashing the power of data. Yet he acknowledges that simply having data is insufficient. Grounding the functionality, Duncan says: "It gives teachers information they need to change their practices to improve student achievement. It shows us when students are making progress and when they're not." Duncan continues by noting that data can be used as part of a school reform agenda, to track student progress from early childhood through to college and careers. Data can determine if students are on track in terms of projected learning and performance. Data can also be used to identify effective and ineffective educators as well as determine if policy changes are needed.

Duncan (2009d, 2012a, 2012b) further believes that educators must be armed with data and that "data matter," saying, "I am a deep believer in the power of data to drive our decisions. Data gives us the roadmap to reform. It tells us where we are, where we need to go, and who is most at risk" (Duncan, 2009a). Yet he also acknowledges that data may not be sufficient. "Data may not tell us the whole truth, but it certainly doesn't lie."

Similarly, Easton (2009, 2010) and Neild (2013) see data and data analysis as powerful tools that must be used to improve schools. Easton (2010) notes that education is "awash in an ocean of data." However, targeted data can and must be used to address pressing educational questions. Neild (2013) has advocated for data use at the state and district levels for all decisions to improve the educational process, requiring the Regional Education Laboratories to help education agencies use data to inform decisions.

So why do data matter? Teachers make hundreds of decisions daily and they are "hungering for data to inform what they do," according to Duncan (2009a, 2011), from in-the-moment decisions to more long-term ones.

> Our best teachers today are using real-time data in ways that would have been unimaginable just five years ago. They need to know how well their students are performing. They want to know exactly what they need to do to teach and how to teach. It makes their job easier and ultimately much more rewarding. They aren't guessing or talking generalities anymore. They feel as if they're starting to crack the code. (Duncan, 2009a)

However, all educators, as well as parents, students, elected officials, and other stakeholders need to understand data (Duncan, 2009a), and many do not. It is a major challenge in the field of education in terms of practice, communicating with the public, and preparing educators to be data literate. Perhaps one of the most pressing issues is that teacher preparation programs do not address the issue of data literacy. Duncan insists that schools of education must step up to the plate and begin to train teachers and other educators how to use data (2012a). He notes that teachers are "not taught how to use data to differentiate and improve instructions and boost student learning" (Duncan, 2009c). If teaching students effectively is to be founded on evidence-based knowledge, teacher preparation programs must begin to introduce such practices along with their content and professional courses (Duncan, 2010b). Policy introduced in 2014 includes steps to improve teacher preparation programs (Teacher Preparation Issues, 2014; U.S. Department of Education, 2014; White House, 2014).

## Funding and Legislation

It is clear from the comments by these three education leaders that high-level education officials not only believe in data, but insist that educators must become data-driven and evidence-based. Having this kind of emphasis is essential and necessary, but it is not sufficient. Simply saying that something like data use must happen does not make it a reality. As we note in Chapter 7, the issue of creating a data-literate education workforce is highly complex and systematic, with many players who must do their part. Interestingly, at one of the SLDS conferences where Secretary Duncan had made a passionate speech about the importance of data and had begun to accept questions, Ellen Mandinach posed the following question about data literacy, couched within the context of the expenditures for the SLDSs: Given that over $500 million had been expended on developing the states' technological infrastructure at that time (then $618 million by 2012 and over $722 million in 2015 [NCES, 2015b]), what has the U.S. Department of Education done to address the human infrastructure issue, recognizing that the prior expenditures would go for naught if educators did not know how to use the data systems and use data more generally? The Secretary thought about the question, but did not have a good answer. This is problematic. There is no federal funding source to help educators at the state and local levels learn to use data. A small number of states (e.g., Arizona and Virginia) are now attempting to introduce policies and funding to provide different models of preparation, but these efforts are contingent on obtaining funding (Canada, Dawson, & Bell, 2015).

Despite the lack of direct funding, data-driven decision making has become a foundational part of education legislation. Data use and the SLDSs are one of the four pillars of the American Recovery and Reinvestment Act of 2009 (ARRA, 2009). Competitions for the Regional Education Laboratories (Institute of Education Sciences, 2011) and the Comprehensive Centers (U.S. Department of Education, 2012) have both included data use and building the capacity of educators to use data as major components of the work. But this work depends on whether data use rises to a high enough level of priority. The inclusion of data-driven concepts into such broad funding efforts is a culmination of a growing emphasis on evidence-based practice over the past decade. The most recent competition for the SLDSs (NCES, 2015a) included, as one of the six foci for future development, educator talent management as a way to address the data literacy issue. But these efforts do not have a broad level of impact in terms of building the capacity of educators to use data. More needs to be done at the state and federal levels to address this issue.

## How Professional Organizations Influence Data-Driven Decision Making

Several professional organizations are relevant to the discussion about data literacy for teachers because they set standards or infuse communication about the importance of the skills and knowledge needed by teachers and teacher candidates. Some create policy; others influence change by working with members to modify practice. Those most directly involved are the Council for the Accreditation of Educator Preparation (CAEP), the American Association of Colleges for Teacher Education (AACTE), National Board for Professional Teaching Standards (NBPTS), and the National Association of State Directors of Teacher Education and Certification (NASDTEC). Past and present leaders of these organizations have entered into the dialogue about data literacy, which we consider a positive thing.

The first indication of the seriousness with which the organizations were considering or taking action on data use came from the National Council for Accreditation of Teacher Education (NCATE), the predecessor to CAEP. NCATE (2010) convened a Blue Ribbon Panel that produced a white paper focusing on the clinical preparation of teachers, a document that Secretary Duncan (2010b) endorsed. One of the NCATE (2010) paper's 10 recommendations was for teacher preparation programs to systematically collect data for the purpose of continuous improvement. Data are seen as providing "robust evidence on teaching effectiveness, best practices, and preparation program performance" (p. 6). In addition, the paper's third recommendation outlines the need for data to be used to judge teacher candidates' progress:

> Candidates' practice must be directly linked to the InTASC core teaching standards for teachers and Common Core Standards, and evaluation of candidates must be based on students' outcome data, including student artifacts, summative and formative assessments; data from structured observations of candidates' classroom skills by supervising teachers and faculty; and data about the preparation program and consequences of revising it. (p. 5)

The fourth recommendation stipulates that teachers must use data to inform their practice, impact their instruction, and monitor student progress. As noted above, these recommendations have become part of the policy to improve teacher preparation programs.

In 2011, when we convened our first meeting of experts about what schools of education could do to address the data literacy human capacity issue, the presidents of AACTE (Sharon Robinson), NCATE (Jim Cibulka), and NBPTS (Joe Aguerrebere) all were in attendance and made clear their views that teachers need to be able to use data (Mandinach & Gummer, 2011). This message has been delivered in other venues. Aguerrebere (2009) served on a panel, convened by the Alliance on Excellent Education, to lay out why teachers must use data in their practice. Cibulka (2013) participated

in a webinar for the Alliance on Excellent Education, where he highlight-
ed the Interstate Teacher Assessment and Support Consortium (InTASC,
2013a, 2013b) standards (described below), noting the importance of data
skills among the standards' knowledge, skills, and dispositions. Robinson
(Mandinach & Robinson, 2014) participated in a Data Quality Campaign
national event, *Empowering Teachers with Data: Policies and Practices to
Promote Educator Data Literacy* (2014a), where she discussed integrating
data literacy into teacher preparation with Ellen Mandinach. Robinson,
however, recognized the many challenges for teacher preparation programs
as they begin to consider integrating data literacy into their curricula.

CAEP gave an invited speaker session for the Graduate Student Council at the 2015 annual convention of the American Educational Research
Association entitled *Data and Assessment Literacy in Schools of Education* (Breaux & Chepko, 2015). In September of 2015 (and again in March
2016) Mandinach gave a workshop at CAEP's annual conference for deans,
associate deans, and assessment directors about data use and data literacy
for teachers. Entitled *Using Data for Programmatic Continuous Improvement and the Preparation of Data Literacy for Educators* (Mandinach &
Gummer, 2015), the workshop had two objectives: (a) to provide guidance
to the audience about how schools of education could use data to inform on
the continuous improvement of their programs; and (b) to help the audience
understand the importance of integrating data literacy into the curricula and
how that might be accomplished. These events indicate that CAEP is serious about data literacy. More than rhetoric, they are intended to stimulate
change through explicit policy and accountability.

NBPTS also continues to be interested in data literacy, but with a less
direct approach. As president until 2015, Ronald Thorpe took two actions
around data literacy. A direct step was to include data literacy, along with
assessment literacy, as one of the core components of the revised assessments.
Candidates for Board certification will have to demonstrate data and assessment literacy. Mandinach was a member of the expert panel for that component. A less direct, but still compelling, step was in communications about
teachers and residency or clinical practice. Thorpe (2014) stressed the need
for learning experiences in teams with a capable mentor, yet recognized that
teacher preparation does not value collaboration, a skill we see as a habit of
mind. According to Thorpe, for teaching to become a true profession, it must
behave like a profession. It must be evidence-based. This must become true of
education as well. As Thorpe noted, there is more to teaching than knowing
content and pedagogy. Teachers must be able to flexibly adapt to the changing
needs of students and classroom circumstances, based on evidence that they
collect that provides indications of what needs to be done.

Other organizations have published documents relevant to the data literacy conversation. The Council of Chief State School Officers (CCSSO)

is a membership organization that focuses state actions to improve public education. CCSSO (2012) published a report titled *Our Responsibility, Our Promise: Transforming Educator Preparation and Entry into the Profession*. The report was informed by the work of a task force that consisted of nine chief state school officers, two individuals from the National Governors Association, and three board members from the National Association of School Boards of Education. The report contains a section about data literacy, although it is called "Assessment Literacy." The issue of conflating data literacy and assessment literacy will be addressed later in this chapter. The American Psychological Association convened a task force (Worrell, Brabeck, Dwyer, Geisinger, Marx, Noell, & Pianta, 2014) to examine teacher preparation programs. The task force made clear in one of its 13 recommendations that teacher preparation programs must prepare teacher candidates to use diverse sources of data so that they can evaluate their own performance and the programs can evaluate the progress of their students. Clearly, professional organizations that influence the field of teacher preparation recognize the importance of data literacy and both inform and enable the creation of policy.

## Standards, Licensure, and Tests

Standards and licensure also communicate policy expectations. Examining the standards, licensure requirements, and licensure tests all can provide insights into how the field views data literacy and what is expected of teacher candidates. The documents also can provide a perspective on what skills and knowledge related to data literacy for teachers are missing and still need to be addressed.

*Standards.* Three sets of standards pertain to data literacy. The first set, from CAEP (2013a, 2013b), are the standards for the accreditation of teacher preparation programs. They are relevant for two reasons. First, they apply the principles of data-driven decision making to the collection and analysis of evidence as it pertains to accrediting schools of education. In one document, CAEP (2013b) describes how data must drive decisions about candidates and programs. Second and most relevant to the issue of data literacy are two components of Standard 1, Content and Pedagogical Knowledge. Standard 1.5 states that teacher candidates must be able to use evidence to inform their practice, considering the impact of their decisions and meeting the needs of all students. Standard 1.3 discusses the use of various assessments, but then stipulates that the candidates must be able to "employ analytic skills necessary to inform ongoing planning and instruction, as well as to understand, and help students understand their own, progress and growth" (CAEP, 2013a, p. 16).

The second source of standards is the American Federation of Teachers' (2012) *Raising the Bar: Aligning and Elevating Teacher Preparation and the Teaching Profession*. Three standards pertain to data literacy.

- Expertise in valid and appropriate use of formative and summative assessments; use of empirical evidence to inform teaching and guide student learning.
- Capacity to keenly and systematically observe students singly and in groups in order to determine their needs and interests and adjust pedagogical strategies accordingly.
- Capacity for "adaptive expertise"—that is, the ability to analyze and diagnose teaching and learning problems, reflect on pedagogical choices, choose strategies to address problems, assess results and continuously refine practices in order to meet students' needs. (p. 16)

The first standard focuses on assessment literacy, but introduces the idea of more general evidence. The second principle implies data collection and analysis through observation, a key component of data literacy. The final standard reflects the existence of an inquiry cycle that underlies much of data literacy in term of the transformation of data ultimately into actionable instructional steps.

The third set of standards goes right to the heart of the skills and knowledge that are part of data literacy. In TASC—the Interstate Teacher Assessment and Support Consortium from the Council of Chief State School Officers (CCSSO)—developed the *Model Core Teaching Standards and Learning Progressions for Teachers 1.0* (InTASC, 2013a). The document presents 10 standards that are categorized into Essential Knowledge, Critical Dispositions, and Performances that, according to experts, comprise effective teaching. Before describing the skills of data literacy for teachers found among these standards, two salient points need to be made. First, the standards focus on assessment literacy. The document speaks to the need for improved assessment literacy:

> The core teaching standards recognize that, to meet this InTASC Model Core Teaching Standards and Learning Progressions for Teachers 1.0, expectation, teachers need to have greater knowledge and skill around how to develop a range of assessments, how to balance use of formative and summative assessment as appropriate, and how to use assessment data to understand each learner's progress, plan and adjust instruction as needed, provide feedback to learners, and document learner progress against standards. In addition, teachers need to know how to make decisions informed by data from a range of assessments, including once-a-year state testing, district benchmark tests several times a year, and ongoing formative and summative assessments at the classroom level. They

should be able to make these decisions both independently and in collaboration with colleagues through a process of ongoing learning and reflection. (pp. 4–5)

Second, the document provides an alignment of key cross-cutting themes, one of which is the "use of data to support learning" (p. 51). In our opinion, the sole focus on assessment literacy is shortsighted. We discuss the problem of conflating assessment literacy with data literacy later in this chapter because it is a continuing problem in the field. When key stakeholders such as CCSSO refer to assessment literacy, they send a strong message that the only data relevant to teachers are assessments, and this is most definitely not the case. Yet they include data as a cross-cutting theme.

We examined the knowledge, dispositions, and performance noted in the crosswalk or reference chart and found some substandards noted in the cross-cutting themes that are not about data use. We also found that some key data skills that are found elsewhere among the standards should be considered part of data literacy and the cross-cutting theme. Yet when we conducted a deeper analysis, it was clear that they include many of the skills identified as part of data literacy for teachers. The key issue here is that teachers need many sources of data, not just assessments, so the discussion must be about data literacy.

Three other components of the InTASC document speak to data-driven decision making. First, the document lays out key assumptions about the standards, one of which is a feedback loop where the use of data is explicitly mentioned as part of gathering evidence on learners' responses to instruction. The feedback loop consists of knowing what effective instructional strategies to use, implementing or doing them, using data to gather evidence, reflecting on the evidence, getting feedback, and then making further instructional adjustments. Second, as InTASC lays out the learning progressions for each standard, it includes a discussion, "Strengthen Analysis and Reflection on Practice," on specific topics such as teaching higher-order thinking or the impact on the classroom environment. Each of those progressions is embedded in a culture of collecting data to better understand impact or performance.

Finally, the most explicit endorsement for data use can be found in the learning progressions for Standard 7 (Planning for Instruction) and Standard 9 (Professional Learning and Ethical Practice). Under Standard 7, there are four strategies: (1) "build skill in analysis of data to guide planning," (2) "strengthen analysis and reflection on use of data in planning," (3) "expand skill in high-level data analysis," and (4) "build collaborative skills to improve use of data in planning" (p. 36). These strategies are steeped in data literacy for teachers, including accessing data, organizing data, interpreting data, collaborative data inquiry, providing feedback, analyzing data, instructional adjustments based on data, using multiple sources of data, looking for patterns, instructional planning based on data, and examining data. Standard 9 focuses on many of the same skills, but is geared to the reflective analysis of teachers' practice. Central here are: using data for planning, reflective analysis of practice, keeping data on student growth, identifying questions to guide the reflection about data, gaining knowledge about qualitative and quantitative data analysis, collaboration, and using data to guide practice and collaboration. Clearly, these and other standards are intended as data-driven activities.

The Assessment Standard consists of nine substandards for Performances, seven for Essential Knowledge, and six for Critical Dispositions. All of these individual substandards were deemed part of data literacy. This speaks to the overlap between assessment literacy and data literacy. As is noted below, only a small number of states to date have invoked the InTASC standards. However, as that number grows, so too will the attention paid to data literacy.

*Licensure.* Indications of what skills and knowledge states deem important for effective performance by teachers can be found in state licensure and certification documents. The documents are not only to guide teacher preparation programs in developing their curricula, they are also intended to set the standards that the programs must address in their courses and practical experiences. These documents are produced by state departments of education or related agencies. These agencies belong to NASDTEC, a membership organization of state directors of certification that focuses on the licensure of teachers. Mandinach, Friedman, and Gummer (2015), with the help of NASDTEC, collected and examined the most current documents found on state websites to understand how states view the skills and knowledge of data literacy for teachers. The findings were interesting. We were able to locate the licensure regulations for all but one state (Wyoming had no documentation). Twenty states do not mention data or mention it in a limited way, whereas thirty-one states explicitly deal with data. In contrast, only two states fail to mention assessment. Eight states have a data standard. One state even has an entire document devoted to data literacy (North Carolina Department of Public Instruction, 2013), stating at the beginning: "Data literacy refers to one's level of understanding of how to find, evaluate, and use data to inform instruction" (p. 1). The document continues: "A data-literate person possesses the knowledge to gather, analyze, and graphically convey information and data to support decision-making" (p. 1). We estimated that less than half of the states—twenty-three—address data literacy, whereas thirty-seven states address assessment literacy.

Based on the data literacy skills we have identified as part of data literacy for teachers (see Chapter 3), the states vary widely in the number of skills they address in their regulation documents: fourteen states cite zero to 10 skills; fourteen states cite 11 to 20 skills; twelve states cite 21 to 30 skills; and eleven states cite 31 or more skills. Seven states that use the InTASC standards cite the most skills of data literacy for teachers. A different seven states even lay out a developmental continuum of how the skills differ, ranging from novice to expert.

Our work also specifies the skills and knowledge required in documentation by state. These are the skills most frequently included across states: plan instruction (39 states), use multiple measures and sources of data (39), use data (37), involve stakeholders (36), monitor student performance (36), communicate (34), analyze data (33), evaluate outcomes (33), collect/gather data (32), document/review results (31), modify instruction (29), make decisions (28), collaborate (28), provide feedback (28), adjust instruction (27), and interpret results (26). Many key skills of data literacy for teachers were noted infrequently across the states: use of inquiry (16 states), access/retrieve/find data (14), use data displays and representations (14), organize data (13), assess data quality (13), draw conclusions from data (11), understand patterns and trends (10), examine data (9), use statistics (8), integrate data (6), predict/hypothesize from data (5), and summarize data (4). These skills will be explained more fully in Chapter 3.

The licensure documents provide an interesting perspective on how states view data literacy, yet caveats exist when interpreting them. One state, Wyoming, has no documentation or regulations at all. The District of Columbia actually has a data standard, but it is clearly about assessments, not data more broadly construed. States vary widely in the amount of documentation about their regulations and the specificity with which they outline requisite skills and knowledge. They may include outlines for different grades, content domains, and roles, whereas others may be general. Some states' documents are comprehensive, considered, and explicit; others are less carefully laid out. Some documents may be old and need to be revised. A good example to follow might be Arizona which, in addition to being an InTASC state, has developed a specific data literacy rubric for their schools of education. Specificity matters when laying out the skills. Further, the confusion between data literacy and assessment literacy matters even more. States must be thoughtful in their wording of these documents.

It is also important to note that the inclusion of the skills and knowledge of data literacy for teachers in licensure documentation is not a guarantee that schools of education will include them in their curricula. Although schools of education report that they abide by the licensure requirements when considering their curricula, some requirements may be impossible to follow due to a lack of specificity, too much specificity, obsolescence, or failure to consider research or policy. A question remains about the level of specificity with which these skills are listed and how they can be translated into actionable practice by schools of education and by professional development providers. Some of the documents were over 300 pages long, leaving us to wonder how the preparation programs could actually adhere to everything in the regulations. At the other end of the spectrum, too little specificity may result in ambiguity and an inability to understand the true intent. The documents should serve as guides to inform the practices of schools of education, so it is important that they have a comprehensive and explicit inclusion of the skills of data literacy for teachers. Consequently, providing both state licensure agencies and schools of education with our definition of data literacy for teachers and laying out the associated skills and knowledge may help them make more considered decisions about data literacy.

The Data Quality Campaign (DQC), a nonpartisan advocacy organization for data use, has conducted annual surveys of states to determine their progress on certain elements and actions needed around data systems and effective data use. The DQC (2015b, 2015c) has laid out 10 Essential Elements and 10 Actions. Action 9 addresses the extent to which states are building the human capacity to use data: Implement policies and promote practices to build educators' capacity to use data (DQC, 2011, 2012, 2013, 2014c). As one of the items that are part of Action 9, the survey asks states to report on whether data literacy is part of teacher licensure and certification. Results from the 2013 survey indicated that 29 states report that they include data literacy for certification/ licensure or data literacy training as a requirement for state program approval. According to the survey, 19 states report they have licensure requirements for teachers around data literacy. Improvements were noted for the 2014 survey with 32 states having licensure or program approval requirements and 22 having licensure requirements. Four states did not respond to the 2014 survey, so the numbers might be even higher. Two caveats surround these data. First, the survey is self-reporting. It is sent to the governor's office and then distributed to individuals who can respond to certain parts of the survey. Second, there is an assumption that the respondents know what data literacy is--and this assumption may be inaccurate.

It is clear from our work and that of the DQC that states are beginning to consider data literacy a component necessary for effective teachers, but much more improvement is needed. More states need to come on board. And those states already reporting that data literacy is part of licensure and certification must understand what the construct really entails. Until that happens, data literacy for teachers will not be a fully required part of educators' practice.

**Tests.** Two main tests are being used to assess teachers' knowledge and skills. How they deal with data literacy reflect trends in the field. One is the *Praxis Series,* developed by Educational Testing Service (ETS). The Praxis tests are part of the process of teacher licensure and are required by many states (ETS, 2015b). The second is the edTPA, developed by the Stanford Center for Assessment, Learning and Equity (SCALE), a newer performance assessment that some states are now requiring (Stanford Center for Assessment for Learning and Equity, 2013, 2014).

Praxis has two sets of tests: Praxis Core Academic Skills for Educators and Praxis II Subject Assessments. We have been in conversation with the developers at ETS who have made clear their intention to include data literacy as part of the required competencies in their licensure tests.

Experts at ETS are currently considering a more performance-based and observational set of tests—the *NOTE Assessment Series* (ETS, 2015a)—that will tap more than knowledge, but practice, based on a framework for teaching developed by Sykes and Wilson (2015). The test will be grounded in the high-leverage practices identified by Deborah Ball and her colleagues at the University of Michigan (TeachingWorks, 2015a, 2015b). Although not explicitly stated in the practices, it is clear that data literacy is an underlying component of many of the practices.

edTPA "provides a measure of teacher candidates' readiness to teach that can inform program completion, licensure, and certification decisions, while supporting candidate learning and preparation program improvement" (SCALE, 2013, p. 1). The performance assessment, with 27 versions in different fields, focuses on planning, instruction, and assessment. It is aligned to the InTASC standards (2013a, 2013b) and the CAEP standards (2013a, 2015). The edTPA includes 15 scoring rubrics, many of which contain skills and knowledge that are considered part of data literacy and will be discussed in subsequent chapters. Like the InTASC standards, the edTPA uses the language of assessment with five rubrics that undergird the assessment tasks:

- Analyzing Student Learning
- Providing Feedback to Guide Learning
- Supporting Students' Use of Feedback
- Evidence of Language Use to Support Content Learning
- Using Assessment to Inform Instruction (SCALE, 2013, p. 11)

These tests require teachers to demonstrate their knowledge of a variety of skills and knowledge, including aspects of data literacy. They are concrete activities that can be used as gatekeepers if test takers fail to perform adequately. The consequences for failure or passing are quite clear, and should stimulate teacher preparation programs to ensure that they address the content of those tests.

## Caveats and Controversies About Data-Driven Decision Making

We would be remiss if we did not address some of the controversies about data use. By no means is data-driven decision making a panacea. It is not the answer to all education problems and questions at any level of the educational system. When people talk about problems with data, they are sometimes interpreted as being about the deficits of the students, not the positives. Data do have limitations. For example, when educators talk about behavioral data, the focus tends toward the negative; that is, toward expulsions, demerits, or arrests. But behavior can also be positive. Similarly, data about family circumstances often focus on at-risk factors, but there also can be positives such as parental support. Because discussions around data often skew negative, it is important to consider a balanced approach.

The collection and use of data have increasingly become both essential and controversial. Data-driven decision making has roots in the accountability movement and often is conflated with a "gotcha" mentality or a witch hunt. *Data* is seen as a four-letter word to many educators: Data are to be feared; data are to be eschewed; data are not to be trusted. Some longtime teachers perceive the use of data as a replacement for their many years of practice and substantial experience.

Why do educators fear data? Probably the main reason is possible negative consequences for both teachers and schools of education. Teachers are concerned about how their students' test scores may be used to evaluate them, with consequences that may impact their jobs or their salaries. Schools of education are concerned about the rating system imposed on them by the National Council of Teacher Quality (Greenberg, Walsh, & McKee, 2015). In fact as noted in Chapter 6, a study we conducted about what schools of education are doing to enhance educators' capacity to use data was not only impacted by the rating of the National Council of Teacher Quality (NCTQ) but also by the concern that the findings would have negative consequences for the respondents to our survey (Mandinach, Friedman, & Gummer, 2015). In follow-up calls and emails to deans of the schools of education, we got responses like: "It is another witch hunt"; "you are trying to make us look bad"; "the survey is a gotcha"; "you are part of NCTQ and therefore we won't cooperate"; and "this is an unfair evaluation of our practices." All of these accusations were unfounded, but they show the possible negativism around data.

Data use is also conflated with the testing movement, giving it a bad reputation. Many critics of education firmly believe that students in the United States are overtested. More time is devoted to preparing for and taking tests than on teaching and learning activities. This accusation is not so far-fetched. The undue emphasis on testing has led many critics to equate data with testing as well as with the Common Core Standards (Common Core State Standards Initiative, 2015a). Data and excessive testing may lead to constrained and scripted curricula where teachers are slaves to pacing guides, with no possibility of creativity or flexibility in what and how they teach. In the ideal world, assessment and instruction should become almost transparent, with a tight feedback loop that includes data as the feeder. The public most commonly thinks about state summative assessments and the test prep that goes with the high-stakes programs. The public may not be aware of the increasing emphasis on the formative assessment process where moment-to-moment assessments are made and immediately fed into the teaching and learning process (Heritage, 2010). These data, along with many other sources of data, help provide a comprehensive picture of the students. The public may also see testing data used for inappropriate purposes. SAT scores are regularly posted on Zillow as a proxy for real estate values. Local newspapers report testing and other kinds of data in the public media, often times with inaccuracies in the data or their interpretations.

Part of the issue here, going well beyond the testing movement, reflects fundamental misunderstandings about what data are being collected and how they are being used. In many states, parents have expressed concern that data are being collected on inappropriate topics, such as the number of guns owned by a family or biometrics. People do not want to provide that information because they fear how it will be used and believe it is intrusive and violates individual privacy. These kinds of data are not part of data collections. We urge as much transparency as possible to quell the misunderstandings and suspicion. Parents and other stakeholders also are rightfully concerned about the protection of data confidentiality and privacy. This is a huge issue and has gained much attention given the increasing number of security breaches on commercial websites. There have been breaches to state data systems. There also have been breaches to mobile device apps that educators have innocently downloaded as possible tools to be used in their practice. Technology directors are doing everything possible to prevent such problems. School districts hopefully are trying to provide training on data privacy and confidentiality to educators to minimize the risks. Ideally, there would be some sort of provision for training through human resources departments. But problems are inevitable, just like someone hacking one's eBay account or credit card.

The public also fears that using data will result in shaming. If data are collected on socioeconomic status, homelessness, disabilities, or other challenging circumstances, the concern is that educators will think less of a family or a student. It is essential that educators have sensitivity to the individual circumstances of their students and not use data to create negativity. The point we want to make here is that data use requires educated users and consumers. They include educators who are collecting, analyzing, interpreting, and acting upon data. They also include students, parents, school board members, other officials, and the general public. Educators need to communicate to these stakeholder groups about data security, that is, how to protect data from breaches and how to protect the privacy and confidentiality of the data. They need to be educated consumers of that information. Our focus has been on data literacy for teachers. And we know there still is a long way to achieving universal data literacy for educators. The problem becomes all the more complex with parents, students, and the general public. How do we help them understand information such as a climate survey, the prevalence of bullying, or the myriad of student performance measures, just to name a few topics? Our message: everyone needs to have some level of data literacy.

## THE CONFLATION OF DATA LITERACY AND ASSESSMENT LITERACY: THE IMPORTANCE OF THE DISTINCTION

Education has long considered assessments to be the most important source of data for teachers. And to use assessments, teachers must be assessment literate. That is, they must have at least a foundational knowledge of measurement to be able to develop tests, select assessment instruments, and analyze results. But assessments are not the only source of data that teachers need and use. In fact, they should be just one of many sources of data that are called upon at different times and for different purposes. This has become an especially salient issue, given the current political landscape around testing. A common belief is that testing, particularly standardized testing, has infringed on the teaching and learning process. Teachers simply are devoting too much time to testing and not enough time to instruction. Data from assessments get wrapped up in the controversy.

We maintain that assessments are a key part of the educational process, one in which there must be a tight feedback loop of instruction, assessment and its findings, and refined instruction. But we also maintain that assessments must be one of many sources of data that provide the essential information about students. For teachers to gain a comprehensive understanding of their students, they must use diverse sources of data to inform their practice. This means triangulating among multiple sources of student performance indicators that include tests, quizzes, problem sets, essays, portfolios, speeches, performance tasks, readings, exercises, and just about any other sort of assignment teachers give. Teachers must also go beyond student performance to consider other types of indicators. These may include measures of self-esteem, motivation, perception, attitude, and grit. Knowing about students' affect can be helpful in structuring what goes on in the classroom. Indicators may also include behavior and justice data to understand if students have been in trouble in or out of school, and relevant health data so teachers can make appropriate accommodations available. Attendance data can provide valuable information about health and/or commitment or impediments to education. Family context can help teachers better understand the students and meet their needs. For instance, knowing if a student has a supportive parental environment, has educational resources at home, is in a group home, is in the foster care system, has a parent holding down several jobs or incarcerated, is in a shelter for the homeless, or has an abusive situation can help a teacher understand the circumstances in which the student is living. Even transportation data can be informative: It can tell the teacher if the student has an excessively long ride on the school bus or must rely on public transportation to get to school. The triangulation among these sources of data helps give teachers a comprehensive depiction of their students. A caution exists, though, to not be overzealous and overinclusive, crossing the line to intrusive and inappropriate data collections.

It should therefore be clear that the data teachers should be using are much more than assessment data, and that's why we focus on data literacy, and not assessment literacy. We do, however, consider assessment literacy to be a component of data literacy because teachers do indeed need to know about assessments and their characteristics.

Educators are not alone in potentially confusing the two constructs. Professional organizations have conflated them in both directions—talking about data literacy but calling it "assessment literacy" and talking about assessment literacy when calling it "data literacy." CCSSO's (2012) report *Our Responsibility, Our Promise* is a prime example of the conflation problem. A section of the report with the subtitle "Assessment Literacy" opens with the follwing statement:

> Just as educator preparation programs must use data to do a better job of preparing candidates and to make changes to their curriculum, assessments, and clinical practice, teachers must also know how to use data to drive instruction. (p. 11)

The report then uses a quote from a National Council of Teacher Quality report about using many sources of data, assessments and other data, and posits NCTQ's three domains of preparation for assessment literacy: assessment literacy, analytic skills, and instructional decision making (NCTQ, 2012). Although the emphasis is on the use of assessments by teachers, the fact that they also describe the importance of using other sources of data is quite telling. The message and the terminology are confused and confusing. Still, it is clear that NCTQ's focus is on assessments:. They talk about measuring and analyzing student performance and planning subsequent instruction *through assessments*.

Another example of the conflation was found in the summer of 2014 when AACTE ran the following series of webinars on assessment literacy:

- The Domain of Assessment Literacy and the Status of Teacher Education Programs—July 7, 2014
- Incorporating Assessment Literacy in Teacher Preparation Programs—July 29, 2014
- Performance Assessment and Assessing Teacher Candidates—August 19, 2014

Because of AACTE's influence with teacher preparation programs, the DQC began having conversations about addressing the conflation head on in a public arena. On July 21 the DQC presented a webinar entitled *What's the Difference Between Assessment Literacy and Data Literacy?* (Data Quality Campaign, 2014d; Mandinach, Kahl, Parton, & Carson, 2014). This session provided an open forum addressing the misconceptions and the need to think about data more broadly. It followed on the heels of the DQC's (2014c) white paper, *Teacher Data Literacy: It's About Time,* which posits the following definition:

> Data-literate educators continuously, effectively, and ethically access, interpret, act on, and communicate multiple types of data from state, local, classroom, and other sources to improve outcomes for students in a manner appropriate to educators' professional roles and responsibilities. (p. 1)

This report was released on the same day that the DQC (2014a) convened a national event to discuss data literacy. The event included policymakers, a chief state school officer, legislative education aides, leaders of professional organizations (including AACTE's president, Sharon Robinson), a teacher, and a researcher. The message of data literacy was beginning to spread.

In a final example of the confusion, even education book publishers conflate assessment and data literacy. In 2014 we walked through the exhibits at the American Educational Research Association annual conference to see what was available about data, data use, and data literacy. At one exhibit we found a catalog with a category, Data-Driven Decision Making. Two of the books within the category were clearly about assessment, with "Assessment" prominent in the titles. Yet the same publisher also had a category, Classroom/Student Assessment, which included a book with "Data-Driven Decision Making" in the title. The confusion continues. It is our hope that this volume will clear up the problem.

But even among the knowledgeable, a common terminology still has been elusive. In 2012 when we convened a group of experts, we devised an exercise to determine their perspective on the conflation issue (Mandinach & Gummer, 2012). We gave each attendee laminate circles, one with "assessment literacy" printed on it and one with "data literacy" on it. We then asked them to depict the degree of overlap of the two constructs using Venn diagrams. Three versions of the renderings were made. The first depicted a small degree of overlap, indicating that the constructs were basically different. A second depicted almost a complete overlap with only a small amount of uniqueness for each construct. The final rendering depicted assessment literacy fully embedded within the more general "data literacy" construct. Well over half of the experts opted for the third rendering. Only about 20% opted for the first and second renderings. Even among the experts, there is not complete agreement, but there is a majority who believe assessment literacy is part of data literacy or there is substantial overlap.

We present one last example of the conflation: the Urban Teacher Residency United's (UTRU) *Assessment and Data Literacy Scope and Sequence* (2014). UTRU is a consortium of teacher residency programs. It has taken on the use of data in teacher preparation. They developed the UTRU Data Literate Teacher Continuum that includes: assessment knowledge, assessment literacy, data collection and management, data analysis, and enacting data-driven instruction. Although the continuum is classified as data literacy, the description of the skills along the continuum focuses on assessments. It is only through discussions with staff that it becomes apparent that UTRU's meaning of *assessment* is not just about tests. What they mean is assessments of student performance, assessments of attitude, assessments of motivation, and assessments of other constructs.

But again, this kind of communication creates confusion. It is why we have strived to provide an understandable and useable definition of the construct "data literacy for teachers," as well as its components, skills, knowledge, and habits of mind. We strive to have this serve as a common definition that can promote a broad understanding of what it means for teachers to be considered data literate.

# CHAPTER 3

# The Conceptual Framework for Data Literacy for Teachers

The previous chapter explained the importance of data literacy for teachers (DLFT) from the research and the policy perspectives and also indicated how data use is becoming part of education policy nationally and within the states, especially in the teacher licensure process. But key to improving data literacy for teachers in teachers' initial and ongoing professional development is understanding the specific knowledge, skills, and dispositions we want them to learn and use. This chapter describes our research program of expert panel and document analysis to specifically elicit the knowledge and skills that undergird the construct "data literacy for teachers." We briefly review the methodology by which we developed a conceptual framework and provide one way to represent the framework that has emerged from our work.

When we first started working on a framework to characterize data literacy for teachers, our intent was to inform the development of a suite of instruments that could be used to determine how and if teachers' use of data improves following professional development. We asked ourselves how we could determine the success of our efforts to teach data literacy if we could not measure the change in the teachers' knowledge, skills, and practices of using data to inform instruction as a result of engaging in professional development. What we thought we needed was an operational definition of data literacy for teachers (Bridgman, 1959). An operational definition is one that characterizes something in terms of the measures used to establish its presence or lack thereof; the classic example is temperature being defined as something that is measured by a thermometer. This process of setting an operational definition, works well for temperature but not so well for complex educational constructs, such as data literacy for teachers.

We knew from the research on data use cited in Chapter 1 that the theoretical frameworks that have been developed to inform research, capacity building, and policymaking related to data use are complex and multilayered. But we thought we could develop a framework that would guide research and instrument development if we narrowed the focus of data literacy to address only data literacy for teachers, coherently organized our synthesis of the research and professional development literature plus our data collected through expert panel reflections on data literacy for teachers, and systematically organized how the standards and licensure documents characterize data use. And, from early discussions with deans of schools of education, data literacy researchers, and policy writers, we knew that the development of an operational definition that included a focus on teaching would have to consider the emerging expertise of teachers over the continuum from preservice to master teacher (Mandinach & Gummer, 2011, 2013a).

What our research has resulted in is far less an operational definition than it is a roadmap of the complex suite of knowledge, skills, and dispositions a teacher needs to master in order to be data literate in the classroom. While an operational definition might have helped narrow the construct "data literacy" to simplify instrument development, the theoretical framework we present in this chapter enables us to articulate the breadth of knowledge, skills, and dispositions that are needed and to articulate which aspects of this complex field particular researchers and developers are targeting. It also helps us illustrate data literacy for teachers without a consideration of the complex area of instruction only takes us partway to actively incorporating data into teaching.

## HOW WE DETERMINED THE KNOWLEDGE AND SKILLS NEEDED FOR DATA LITERACY FOR TEACHERS

Working with a panel of experts in data-use research, policy, and professional development provision, which also included former teachers, we explored what we hoped would elicit their thinking of the key elements of data literacy for teachers. We first asked the experts what they thought the terms *data literacy* and *assessment literacy* meant. The beginning of the complexity of data literacy for teachers became immediately apparent as the experts addressed how different stakeholder roles (students, teachers, or administrators) might influence a definition of data literacy for teachers. They also emphasized the importance of a continuum between novice and expert (both teachers and administrators), and articulated the influence of epistemological and social aspects of what counts as data on what is meant by literacy. Their response to the question of what *data literacy* meant was, "It depends."

One researcher, commenting on the difficulty of the task, pointed out that different communities of users define data literacy in quite varied ways. She used the context of sports fans who have a specialized language when making decisions about the relative success of their teams and communicating those results to others. She also pointed out that manifestations of data literacy are mediated by the culture in which they are expressed. For example, data literacy about sports might be more sophisticated in the *New York Post* than in a publication with less emphasis on sports reporting, while data literacy about finance might be more so in *The Wall Street Journal* than in a publication with less of a focus on financial matters.

The experts also indicated that data literacy might be different when viewed from the perspective of education research than from the perspective of teacher practice. When we constructed a Wordle, a process which shows the frequency with which certain terms are represented in the experts' writings, we had a glimpse of the complexity of the topic as shown in Figure 3.1. The diagram shows the plethora of terms that the experts used to define data literacy.

## Review of Professional Development Materials

We also presented the group with our analysis of the topics addressed in 33 commercial texts that data literacy professional development providers use to structure the content and processes around data literacy that they endorse for teachers. We had examined these different texts to determine how they structured information about data or assessment literacy and then developed a coding scheme to identify the relative importance of each topic. There was quite a bit of variability in the topics addressed in the texts. Three categories of topics were found in more than 80% of the texts: the inquiry cycle, different types of data, and the role of data analysis to inform decisions.

In these practitioner texts, the knowledge structure of the data inquiry cycle became very evident as a major way to organize thinking about data literacy, reflecting the importance of the inquiry cycle in the research on data use, especially by administrators (Easton, 2009; Hamilton et al., 2009; Knapp, Copeland, & Swinnerton, 2007; Mandinach, Honey, et al., 2008; Means et al., 2010). The inquiry cycle refers to the recursive way that practitioners identify problems or issues of practice, formalize questions that help specify ways to examine a particular issue, identify and collect data to inform those questions, act on the data to identify potential antecedents or causes of the problem or issue, and then decide how to act on solutions that emerge. An evaluative process typically rounds out the inquiry cycle before the current problem being studied is re-examined or a new issue emerges.

For example, during the summer curriculum planning sessions, a group of mathematics teachers at a particular grade level might be gathered into a data team wherein they could collaboratively examine particularly difficult areas of student learning that are persistently resistant to improvement. From the end-of-year test results, they know that students have difficulty with division of fractions. They refine the question of what it is about division of fractions that presents students with the difficulty. They examine what it is that the students need to know and be able to do to be ready to

**Figure 3.1. Wordle of Data Literacy Definitions**

learn about division of fractions, and examine the performances of their incoming students on district assessments from the previous year. They step back and consider other types of data that might help them understand who did not do well in those areas and what they might also consider beyond just planning specific classroom interventions for the whole class and for specific groups of learners.

During the school year, the data teams meet iteratively to examine how students are doing on specific lessons that lead up to the unit on division of fractions. Their examination of data expands to include attendance and behavioral data that contribute to students' readiness to learn. They design specific assignments and assessments that provide an audit trail of student learning that informs them about the ways in which the students are experiencing what the teachers are providing to them in instruction. The inquiry cycle goes from being a broadly defined set of iterative activities at the beginning of the year, where the emphasis is on planning, to a tightly articulated cycle that informs day-to-day planning and implementation of lessons. At the end of the unit on division of fractions, the teachers use evidence from a more summative assessment to evaluate the extent to which they have been successful in helping students learn.

A focus on different types of data that teachers might use was the second-highest-ranking topic in the professional development materials. The third highly ranked topic dealt with the knowledge and skills around data analysis in making inferences and interpretations and informing decisions (Mandinach & Gummer, 2012, 2013b).

The 102 additional topics and subtopics addressed the following topics:

- Precursor conditions to data literacy, including school vision
- Examination of issues of authority, including who has the authority to make particular decisions at the school or classroom level
- Importance of the connection to other initiatives
- Understanding the change or continuous improvement process
- Importance of collaboration
- Focus on equity and cultural proficiency
- Connection of data use with school culture
- Importance of the characteristics of professional development that are needed to engage teachers and educational leaders in addressing data literacy for teaching

Other topics focused more directly on assessment and data, including developing the understanding of types of assessment processes, developing knowledge and skills around data access and quality, and understanding data use/sufficiency. Fewer than half the texts addressed topics around planning to differentiate instruction or to determine specific daily instruction in light of data. Planning in terms of how to shift the implementation of programs and understanding research evidence were the two least-represented topics in the professional development texts.

**Input from the Expert Panels**

The discussions with the panel of experts provided us with additional definitional material about data literacy and the challenges and contextual issues that affect it. The experts agreed on many aspects of data literacy, though they recognized that their terminology was frequently different. They also recognized the importance of a conceptual data literacy framework to support multiple aspects of teacher practice, preparation, policy, and research. We have given an account of the details of these conceptual areas in an earlier report (Mandinach & Gummer, 2012); the general categories included the following:

- Developing or refining professional development models and tools
- Influencing the ways in which data literacy might be introduced and strengthened in programs in schools of education
- Informing a shared research agenda and seeking or providing funding for this research agenda
- Influencing policymakers' views of data literacy

- Informing educator hiring practices
- Assisting in the development of assessments to measure data literacy

The expert sessions also gave us a more nuanced and emergent perspective of data literacy for teachers. The analysis, though, left us with a laundry list of statements about what teachers should know and be able to do. We organized the statements into three focus categories as follows:

- Problem focus
- Data focus
- Process focus by which data are used to inform decisions

A fourth category emerged that consisted of important knowledge and skill statements that the experts invoked that were unlike those in the other three categories. This catch-all category included knowledge and skills around disciplinary areas, a proclivity to use data, and supporting the use of data by students (Mandinach & Gummer, 2013a). This final category spurred our thinking of how we might connect data literacy and teaching.

After we combined the professional development material analysis and the expert panel's input, we ended up with more than 100 sets of knowledge and skill statements to characterize data literacy. We examined the multiple lists for redundancy and close synonyms, which left us with a list of 50 knowledge and skill components that we originally labeled "elements." However, we lacked a way to represent the hierarchical, nested, or linked nature of the knowledge and skill statements.

In Chapter 2 we described how an analysis of the standards, licensure requirements, and licensure tests provide a policy perspective of what characterizes data literacy, and these data also supported a triangulation process we used to refine the conceptual list of knowledge and skills we were developing (Mandinach, Friedman, & Gummer, 2015). We expanded this analysis to include assessment literacy, as our findings indicated that the expert panelists viewed assessment as a component of data literacy (Mandinach & Gummer, 2011, 2013b). We identified 44 sets of knowledge and skills statements (elements) from the analysis of the licensure documents. We then conducted a crosswalk to identify synonyms and conceptually unique statements of knowledge and skills from the 50 elements that emerged from the expert panel and the 44 elements that emerged from the licensure work. We sorted the 59 elements that emerged from the convergence into seven larger "components" of data literacy:

- Inquiry Process
- Habits of Mind
- Data Quality
- Data Properties

- Data Use Procedural Skills
- Transform Data Into Information
- Transform Information Into Decisions

But these seven components did not leave us with a way to incorporate the knowledge and skill statements into a heuristic that communicated the integration of data use into teaching. Our previous research culminated in the development of a tentative conceptual framework that incorporated the tables of knowledge and skills statements into the common heuristic of the inquiry cycle.

### Initial Framework: Integrating Content and Pedagogy with Data Literacy

We continue to struggle with the extent to which there are generic data literacy knowledge and skills or whether certain knowledge and skills are tied directly to the discipline the teacher is teaching. All our sources for the knowledge and skills statements (expert panel evidence, text analysis, and licensure analysis) indicated that data literacy is deeply embedded in other aspects of teaching, such as curriculum planning and instructional implementation.

We also needed a way to connect what we were identifying as sets of teacher knowledge and skills of data literacy with the larger research on teacher knowledge. Shulman's perspective (Shulman, 1987) on teacher knowledge best fits the cognitive perspective that we are addressing using empirical and normative evidence from experts, professional development materials, and licensing standards. His perspectives identify seven areas of teacher knowledge: content knowledge; general pedagogical knowledge; curriculum knowledge; pedagogical content knowledge; knowledge of learners and their characteristics; knowledge of educational contexts; and knowledge of educational ends, purposes, and values. We initially focused on the two Shulman areas of teacher knowledge as being integral to data literacy for teachers, namely, content knowledge and pedagogical content knowledge. Our initial characterization of data literacy for teaching invoked the following aspects of teacher decision making:

- It is situated within the specific content that teachers are addressing as learning outcomes.
- It includes a focus on the use of data to inform teaching.
- It draws heavily on teacher pedagogical content knowledge.

We argue that teachers do not use data to inform teaching without incorporating knowledge and skills that address instructional objectives that focus on the disciplinary areas that they are teaching; reading, mathematics,

**Figure 3.2. Original Organization of Data Literacy Conceptual Framework**

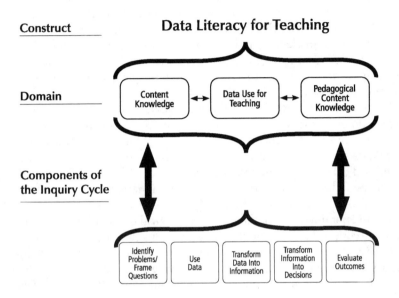

social science, or science. We also argue that data use for teaching is strongly connected to the knowledge and skills that teachers use to translate that content knowledge into appropriate learning experiences for teaching. This is seen in the top part of Figure 3.2.

We also needed a way to think about the overlap of the inquiry cycle for educator decision making and the seven components that resulted from our synthesis of the elements of data literacy for teachers' knowledge and skills. Six of those components were more cognitive in nature, while the Habits of Mind component seemed to reference values and conative aspects of teacher beliefs or dispositions. By *conative*, we mean the ways in which teachers integrate their cognitive perspectives and belief systems in order to produce actions. We originally split the Inquiry Process component into two components, Identify Problems of Practice and Frame Questions, based on our expert panel's perspectives. We merged Data Quality, Data Properties, and Data Use Procedural Skills into one component, Data Use, and kept the components of Transform Data Into Information and Transform Information Into Decisions. Finally, to better fit the inquiry cycle, we added the Evaluate Outcomes component. Because we felt the seventh component, Habits of Mind, was not as cognitively oriented as the other six components and did not fit well within the inquiry cycle, we left it out of this current conceptual framework but will discuss it in Chapter 4.

As an example of this integration, a teacher must combine her understanding of mathematics as a discipline, her understanding of the specific ways in which mathematics content is expressed in math pedagogy (pedagogical content knowledge), and her interpretation of the data that emerged from the teaching context—including assessment, behavior, attendance, and demographic data, among others—to make multiple instructional decisions at different time scales.

Using an inquiry cycle heuristic, the teacher must identify a particular problem that students were having with the multiplication of fractions based on assessment data she collected. She must coordinate that student performance data with attendance and behavior data to determine which students had missed relevant instruction she had already delivered. She would use her understanding of the mathematics content inherent in the topic to focus on aspects of the mathematics that are particularly complex. And she would use her understanding of mathematic pedagogical content knowledge to examine misconceptions or inappropriate solutions the students were using in exercises and problems, as well as to identify specific additional and supplementary classroom activities she could provide for students to get them to reconsider and relearn the content as they think about their understanding of the math.

## Expanding Beyond Content and Pedagogical Content Knowledge

However, as we re-examined Shulman's 1987 characterization of the knowledge base for teaching, we realized we had not included several of his categories in the original framework that had clear connection to data use. They include the "knowledge of learners and their characteristics" (Shulman, 1987, p. 8), which has a strong connection to the inclusion of multiple forms of data beyond just student performance that we think differentiates data literacy from assessment literacy (Mandinach, Friedman, & Gummer, 2015). Shulman articulates two additional categories of the knowledge base for teaching that we think also have strong connections to data, including the "knowledge of educational contexts, ranging from the workings of the group or classroom, the governance and financing of school districts, to the character of communities and cultures" and "knowledge of educational ends, purposes, and values, and their philosophical and historical grounds" (Shulman, 1987, p. 8). We have included "general pedagogical knowledge" and "curriculum knowledge," as these knowledge categories are likely to be invoked as teachers use data to inform their teaching. This has expanded our notion of data literacy for teachers so that Figure 3.3 is a better representation of our current framework.

**Figure 3.3. Revised Conceptual Framework for Data Literacy for Teachers**

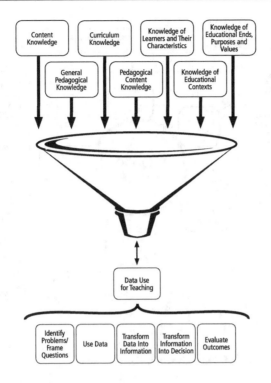

## THE COMPONENTS AND ELEMENTS OF DATA LITERACY FOR TEACHERS

The conceptual framework we developed articulates the elements of data literacy for teaching that are included in each of the components identified as part of an inquiry cycle. The inquiry cycle describes a process of moving from (1) *identification of a problematic issue*, to refining that issue into a question or set of questions that can be examined empirically. As the issue or problem becomes more clearly defined, teachers must identify and (2) *use data* that might illuminate and refine what the problems are. The process describes the need to interpret and draw inferences from the data to (3) *transform data into information.* Teachers then must (4) *transform information into decisions* to identify and implement a potential solution to the problem or issue. The final component of the cycle is to (5) *evaluate the outcomes* of the inquiry cycle work when the solution is implemented. While this form of educational decision making is described as a cycle, it might be better characterized as an iterative spiral of empirical decision making that has multiple potential feedback loops and interconnections. This process connects the components of the domain, "Data Use for Teaching," shown in the conceptual framework in Figure 3.3 and in the knowledge representation in Figure 3.4.

**Figure 3.4. Domain of Data Use for Teaching**

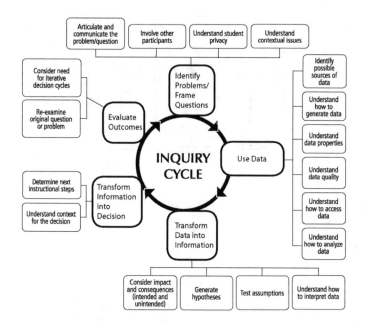

## One Representation of Data Literacy For Literacy

A knowledge representation provides an embodiment of the domain in such a way that essential elements of the domain may be brought into focus to support collaborative discourse about the study of a phenomenon. This embodiment also highlights a potential weakness of a knowledge representation in that what is not represented may not be studied. A complex domain of data literacy for teachers likely will have multiple knowledge representations that identify different components and relationships that serve different purposes. In our earlier publication in *Teachers College Record* (Gummer & Mandinach, 2015), we presented our initial domain analysis of data literacy for teachers.

We use the domain analysis of data literacy for teachers to examine the ways in which Shulman's (1987) seven categories of knowledge are leveraged through the lens of "data use for teaching" to inform decisions about what and how to teach. Our framework of the domain of data literacy for teachers through the heuristic of the inquiry cycle examines the requisite knowledge and skills in a potential hierarchical relationship as follows:

Components—the main aspects of the inquiry cycle
Subcomponents—large-grain sets of knowledge and skills

Elements—finer-grain statements of knowledge and skills
Subelements—finest-grain statements that may include
synonyms

Our current representation of data literacy for teachers is presented in
Figures 3.4 through 3.7. Figure 3.4 shows the component and subcompo-
nent levels of knowledge and skills, while Figures 3.5 through 3.7 expand
the element and sub-element levels of four components: Use Data, Transform Data Into Information, Transform Information Into Decisions, and
Evaluate Outcomes. We chose this quasi-concept map as an alternative to
lists of knowledge and skills in a table or in bullets. The map allows us to
consider the cross-component iterations that teachers and data coaches have
indicated to us are an essential element of the way in which they use data to
inform instructional decisions.

## Identify Problems and Frame Questions Component

The first component of the "Data Use for Teaching" domain, Identify Prob-
lems/Frame Questions, illustrated in Figure 3.4, identifies the knowledge
and skills that are necessary to take a poorly defined problem of practice
and turn it into a question or set of questions that can be examined empirically. Implicit to our framework is the premise that decisions are made
rationally and based on information. And throughout our framework, the
importance of communication skills is highly relevant. Getting the problem
or issue into a commonly defined and articulated set of *issues or questions*
requires understanding of the *contextual issues* at the student, school, and
district level. Contextual issues include the nature of the student body, the
number and types of initiatives, and the authority structure of the school or
district.

Teachers need to know how to *involve other participants*, such as non-
teaching professionals in their schools, parents, and, increasingly, students
themselves. This component requires that the individuals undertaking the
inquiry know who else needs to be involved in articulating the problem
in order to arrive at a well-framed question that can be investigated. We
added *understanding student privacy* issues to the initial step of the inquiry
process to underscore its importance throughout data literacy for teachers.
Teachers need to *understand student privacy issues* from multiple perspectives, including what is required of them by the Family Educational Rights
and Privacy Act (FERPA), that legally protects the privacy of student education records, or the Health Insurance Portability and Accountability Act
(HIPAA), that legally protects privacy of individually identifiable health information, or relevant state or local regulations and how student privacy
operates within the classroom setting, the school environment and in public
(Mandinach, Parton, et al., 2015).

## Use Data Component

We label the next component of the inquiry cycle Use Data, recognizing that the label of this conceptual component is still quite generic. Figure 3.5 shows the elements and subelements for this component.

This component represents the process by which teachers move from initially articulating a teaching issue and the questions by which that issue can be examined to identifying and examining data to inform their work. Figure 3.5 shows the multiple subcomponents and their associated elements and sub-elements that define the complex component of Use Data. Two large subcomponents include Identify possible sources of data and Understand how to generate data. In order to identify possible sources of data, teachers need to know that *different data have different purposes.* Teachers need to understand the *appropriate level of data* to examine the particular questions they are trying to answer. Student problems with multiplying fractions cannot be informed by student scores on standardized tests, even if information on particular items from those tests is available at the student level. Such data might be more useful to inform programmatic decisions of curricular scope and sequence throughout the school year.

However, not all necessary and useful data will be immediately available for teachers, so they need to *understand assessment* by *developing sound assessment design and implementation practices* and *using formative and summative assessments* appropriately in their practices. By sound practices, we mean that teachers need to identify and develop fair, reliable, and valid assessments. Understanding what is meant by fairness (or lack of bias) in assessment, and what is important to know about reliable and valid assessment in the context of the classroom as opposed to understanding those characteristics of good assessment in more standardized contexts, is another conceptual area where the required knowledge and skills are multiple and complex (Stiggins, 2002). As we have indicated above, assessment literacy is a complex construct that we include in data literacy for teachers, and multiple volumes have been written about how to help teachers develop the knowledge and skills associated with developing and implementing both formative and summative assessments (Chappuis, Stiggins, Arter, & Chappuis, 2009).

Teachers need to *understand data properties* to know what counts as appropriate and valid data. This element could unpack into a very complex area of multiple additional concepts and skills as we don't know how much knowledge teachers really need in order to understand validity in education data. Teachers also need to *use quantitative and qualitative data* as needed in order to move beyond a focus on just numbers associated with student assessment performance. *Understanding the specificity of data to a particular question* refers to the knowledge and skills teachers must have to understand that some data can address the issue being examined, while other

**Figure 3.5. Elements of Data Use**

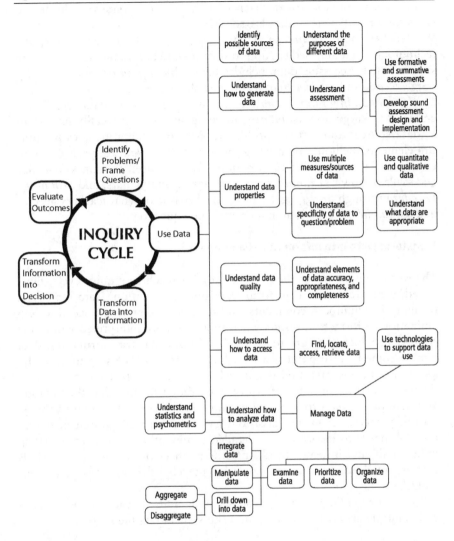

data will not. Finding the applicable data for a given issue is complex, and it is also important both to *understand what data are appropriate* in a given context, and which are not.

*Understanding data quality* is another concept that has different levels of knowledge and skills for the classroom teacher context than it does for standardized assessment or data use by administrators. What teachers need in order to *understand data accuracy, appropriateness, and completeness* may or may not be addressed in a course in basic statistics. Surely teachers need to be able to identify inaccurate, misleading, or out of range data, but to what extent do the statistics typically taught in educational psychology or assessment courses provide teachers with the appropriate knowledge and skills for what they do in the classroom?

Teachers need to *understand how to access data,* particularly as the technologies that are used to support data use are becoming more and more sophisticated. Accessing data includes being able to *find or locate data, arrange access,* and *retrieve data* from multiple locations.

*Understanding how to analyze data* is at the heart of data use. Teachers need to know how to *manage data;* again this is especially important as data sources and systems proliferate. Managing data includes multiple sub-elements including *organizing and prioritizing data* to get it ready to transform into actionable information. Teachers need to gain knowledge and skills of how to *examine data,* to *integrate, manipulate,* and *drill down into data* through disaggregation. Again, the issue of what teachers need to *understand in statistics* is an important, open question.

### Transform Data Into Information Component

The third component of the data literacy for teachers inquiry cycle, illustrated in Figure 3.6, is Transform Data Into Information. Data represents the empirical numbers, comments, and statements that are provided for examination. Information results when those data are interpreted within the context in which they are to be used. Without that transformation, data remain something to point towards, but not act on. The step from analysis of data to interpretation is not well defined. How teachers move from their examination of data, prioritize what they use and what they ignore, and manipulate data to generate meaning in the context related to the issues they encounter in the classroom has not been well examined. Future research needs to incorporate a detailed examination of teachers working individually and in teams to identify the nuances of knowledge and skills that are involved. The current research on teacher decision making has not had that focus.

As shown in Figure 3.6, to make meaning of data, teachers need to activate multiple areas of knowledge and skills, including the following:

- Understand data displays and representations
- Assess patterns and trends
- Probe for causality (by generating hypotheses that represent causal reasoning)
- Synthesize diverse data
- Summarize and explain data
- Articulate inferences and conclusions

**Figure 3.6 . Elements of Transform Data Into Information**

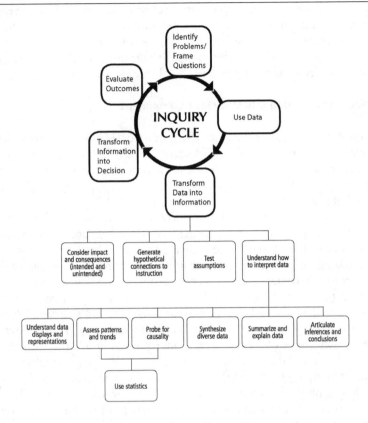

What teachers need to know and to be able to do to examine possible relationships between and among data and instructional contexts in order to consider *test assumptions* of particular issues, such as problematic student performances, have not been well characterized. For instance, a group of students' low performance on an assessment might be because they don't understand the material they experienced in the current lesson. Alternatively their lack of understanding might point to a more fundamental gap in their knowledge in a lesson a month or a year previously. On the other hand, the students might have been absent from school or class when the lessons were provided. While teachers are encouraged to consider root causes of particular problematic performances, the nature of that causal reasoning is not well examined as they *generate hypothetical connections to instruction.*

Teachers use their understanding of the context of classroom learning to *consider the impact and consequences (intended and unintended)* of using data that are analyzed and interpreted in particular ways on their classroom practices and the learning experiences of their students. For instance, any decision to divide students into groups and provide remedial instruction to one group changes those students' opportunity to learn what the rest of the class experiences. In contrast, teachers can no longer just march through a scope and sequence of curricular materials without considering what a gap in student understanding might mean for future learning.

### Transform Information Into Decisions Component

The fourth component of the Data Use inquiry cycle begins to more directly demonstrate the overlap of the seven categories of Shulman knowledge with data use for teaching. In the component shown in Figure 3.7 where teachers *transform information into decisions*, teachers are applying multiple types of knowledge and skills.

How teachers *understand the context for the decision* includes knowledge of the learning objectives, content, and the curriculum (what comes next or later in the scope and sequence). They also bring into action their understanding of pedagogy and pedagogical content knowledge to *determine next instructional steps*. Teachers need to know how to move beyond using data to *monitor student performances*, which only measures whether or not the students have learned, so that they can *diagnose what students need*. When they *make instructional adjustments*, they examine how they might reteach a given lesson or teach the next lesson in order to help students make sense of the previous one. This is more about the teaching aspect of data literacy for literacy than it is about the data aspect, and multiple verbs that apply to instructional planning arose in our analyses. Teachers make instructional decisions on multiple levels, both within the context of a particular lesson and across lessons and units. Teachers also use what they know about the students and their characteristics, their knowledge of educational ends (such as standards), and their understanding of their own school contexts to decide what happens next for students to better *understand the context for a decision*. As they *determine next steps*, they decide whether all of the data they have collected and analyzed still do not give them adequate information to make deviations from what they might have already planned and use the data to monitor students while they proceed. Alternatively, they may have sufficient information so they can actually diagnose what the potential reasons are for the student issues and actually make instructional adjustments.

### Evaluate Outcomes Component

The final component of the data literacy for teachers inquiry cycle is the knowledge and skills teachers use when they *evaluate the outcomes* of the decisions (see Figure 3.7). At this stage, they *consider the need for iterative*

**Figure 3.7. Elements of Transform Information Into Decisions and Evaluate Outcomes**

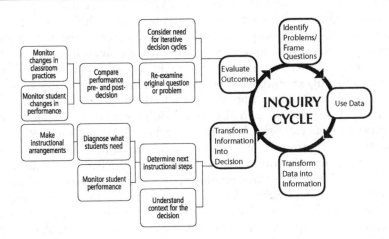

*decision cycles* as they *re-examine the original question or decision*. This step requires teachers to use the knowledge and skills presented in earlier components, as they identify and collect additional data to *compare performances pre- and post-decision*. Those data reflect the need to *monitor student changes in performance* and to *monitor changes in classroom practices* to ensure that the instruction was implemented as intended in the decision. Throughout the evaluation stage of the inquiry process, teachers need to determine any unintended consequences to be able to conclude that the initial issue that started the inquiry cycle has either been adequately addressed or needs revisiting. Unintended consequences at the classroom level might include engendering additional misconceptions as teachers choose an inappropriate instructional sequence to attempt to address gaps in learning.

## OPEN INVITATION FOR DIALOGUE ON DATA USE FOR TEACHING

We do not present this representation of "Data Use for Teaching" as the only way that the underlying knowledge and skills can be characterized, nor is this a finished representation. In fact, Edith Gummer regards the diagram as a way to illustrate the "hot mess we have with data use in education." We are working at an intermediate level of consideration that we hope will integrate research, such as some researchers' studies relative to what teachers need to know and do around student privacy, with other researchers' studies relative to teacher understanding of aspects of data quality. We are advocating for research and professional development practices that go beyond the knowledge and skills to use data and transform it into information to connect to what actually happens in the classroom.

As described here, we realize that the concepts of "data," "literacy," and "teaching" were individually complex. When combined, they represented an even more complex set of constructs that made the development of a framework both necessary and hard to do. However, as the next chapter discusses, we have come to recognize that a domain analysis of knowledge and skills that characterize data use for teaching does not provide sufficient categories to truly capture what people should know and be able to do to be successful practitioners who use data effectively. A simple identification of the cognitive areas of knowledge and skills is unlikely to capture the complexity of the teachers' data use in practice. An epistemic frame, used as the theory of learning that supports the development of simulations and educational games (Shaffer et al., 2007) provides a richer set of categories. They include knowledge (the declarative, procedural schematic, and strategic elements of a data literacy for teachers) and skills (the actions that people have to be effective in doing in using data for teaching) explicated above. But data literacy for teachers also includes values (the beliefs that people hold about a conceptual and practice area of teaching), identity (the way that people see themselves as members of a community acting in a domain), and epistemology (the warrants that connect evidence to claims or actions within a practice) (Shaffer et al., 2007). The next chapter examines what we need to consider about values, beliefs, and dispositions around data literacy for teachers.

# CHAPTER 4

# Beyond Knowledge and Skills

## Examining Values, Beliefs, and Dispositions Toward Data Use

As we described in the previous chapter, characterizing the knowledge and skills that teachers need to effectively use data to inform teaching, what we call data literacy for teachers (DLFT), is complex and crosses multiple domains of knowledge related to teaching. However, examining the cognitive aspects of data literacy for teachers is not sufficient. As we have engaged in our research program that examines how experts, researchers, professional development providers, state education agencies, and others characterize data literacy for teachers, we consistently identified a number of statements about data use that didn't fall easily into a cognitive framework indicating what a teacher should know and be able to do. For example, statements such as "Having data-focused habits of mind" (or dispositions toward using data) and "Believing in data use" did not easily fit into the framework we established in Chapter 3.

Aside from identifying statements associated with data literacy for teachers that did not fit the components of the inquiry cycle articulated in Chapter 3, this chapter discusses what might be called the "noncognitive aspects of teaching," those "habits of professional action and moral commitments that underlie the performances [that] play a key role in how teachers do, in fact, act in practice" (InTASC, 2013a, p.6). Without these components, articulating data literacy for teachers remains an intellectual exercise unconnected to the core human element of teaching.

This chapter presents our current thinking about those values, beliefs, and dispositions toward data, based on relevant research findings. We do not think that they are affective perspectives of data use: perspectives focusing on how teachers feel about using data or their emotional reactions toward the use of data. Rather, we think that these noncognitive components represent the *conative* framing of domain. By that, we mean that values, beliefs, and dispositions toward data represent how teachers integrate their beliefs about data use for teaching with their knowledge and skills to support the actions that they take. For the sake of simplicity, we describe these noncognitive components as "data-oriented beliefs and dispositions," as we feel that these characterize a number of values and beliefs that make up the moral aspects of teaching (Hansen, 2001).

The relative brevity of this chapter is not intended to indicate that the noncognitive components of data literacy for teachers outlined below are less important than the knowledge and skills described at length in Chapter 3. We see them as fundamentally different. The brief treatment is more a function of the credible evidence that supports the various components. Put simply, these beliefs and dispositions may not have the empirical evidence that support their characterization as "knowledge" (Fenstermacher, 1994), whereas substantial research has contributed to the delineation of the framework presented in Chapter 3. We see the noncognitive components as a work in progress that requires more research attention.

## RESEARCH FINDINGS ON TEACHERS' BELIEFS ABOUT DATA USE

Research on teachers' beliefs and dispositions about data use is only beginning to emerge. The work of Dunn and colleagues (Dunn, Airola, & Garrison, 2013; Dunn, Airola, Lo, & Garrison, 2013a, 2013b) demonstrates the intersection of the knowledge and skills captured in our cognitive framework and the beliefs and concerns teachers have about their use of data. Dunn and colleagues (2013b) developed and validated survey instruments they used to measure the improvements in teachers' concerns and efficacy in data use during professional development in data use sponsored by the Oregon Department of Education. Their focus was on the intensity of teachers' concerns about data use and their efficacy in data-driven decision making. The researchers developed three instruments to get at this tripart model, including the Data-Driven Decision Making (DDDM) Knowledge Test, a Stages of Concern Questionnaire (SoCQ)for data-driven decision making based on the work of Hall, George, and Rutherford (1979), and the DDDM Efficacy Assessment (3D-MEA). The knowledge measure is the least developed of the three instruments and little information is available about that aspect of the model.

Operating from the social learning theory of Bandura (1977), the researchers examined teachers' beliefs that they can use data effectively to inform decision making in the classroom and their concerns or anxieties around that use (Dunn et al., 2013b). Dunn and colleagues (2013a) focused on classroom level data-driven decision making (DDDM) and used that term for teachers' processes in identifying "patterns of performance that reveal student academic strengths and weaknesses relative to established learning goals and the planning of instructional practices to support academic success for all students" (p. 87). Through exploratory and confirmatory factor analysis, the researchers identified four aspects of teachers' use of data at the classroom level that included their ability to access data and select appropriate reports and to use technology-based data systems. They also considered teachers' skills in interpreting and evaluating findings from the analysis of data for instructional decisions, as well as their anxiety related to engaging in data-use practices. Using a 5-level Likert scale, the 3D-MEA includes 22 items addressing anxiety for data-driven decision making and four types of efficacy. Further analysis indicated that the construct of efficacy for data analysis, interpretation, and use for instructional decision making was actually two different constructs that separate teachers' beliefs in their skills for successfully analyzing and interpreting student data from their beliefs about their abilities to connect data interpretation to what happens next in the classroom (Dunn et al., 2013b).

The work of Dunn and her collaborators corroborates the findings from qualitative studies of teachers' self-efficacy with respect to the use of data at the classroom level indicating that teachers tend to possess low levels of confidence in their ability to engage in DDDM (Bettesworth, Alonzo, & Duesbery, 2008). However, much of the data from Bettesworth and colleagues were collected through the use of a Likert type of survey for which no technical quality information exists.

This research illuminates certain aspects of teachers' beliefs and dispositions about data literacy for teachers. However, the perspective of efficacy and concerns for data use does not provide us with a framework that we can use to articulate the noncognitive components of data literacy for teachers.

## BELIEFS AND DISPOSITIONS:
## ESSENTIAL SUPPORTS FOR DATA LITERACY FOR TEACHERS

The concept of "self-efficacy" doesn't address the underlying beliefs and dispositions that were characterized by our expert panels from whom we elicited perspectives of data literacy for teachers or by the state standards for teacher licensing and accrediting that we reviewed in Chapter 3. After we organized the key statements from these analyses into the inquiry cycle components of data literacy for teachers, we were left with some overarching conceptual areas that did not fit easily into the knowledge and skills framework. However, we felt these concepts were important to support the research and development agendas of data literacy for teachers for researchers, professional development materials and providers, and other interested parties. In many ways, these concepts address the heart of data literacy for teachers. To fully understand data literacy for teachers, we need to ascertain how teachers embody these beliefs and dispositions in their own characterization of themselves as teachers and in their practices.

## All Students Can Learn

Without the *belief that all students can learn*, a teacher has little need or few concerns to use data effectively to address the learning of all of his or her students. Holding a mindset that some students do not have the cognitive capacity or the necessary support structures to learn provides a belief that a teacher can use to avert a substantive identification and examination of why some students do not perform well in the classroom or on standardized tests. Alternatively, a teacher holding this belief might use data to confirm the differential status of learners rather than using data to identify where and how to support learning. Holding this perspective implicitly may lead to less than productive interactions in a data team or professional learning community. This is a foundation belief that undergirds data literacy for teachers.

## Belief in Data Use to Inform Teaching

Parallel to the above is a *belief in the use of data to inform teaching*. If the teacher has the perspective that teaching is an art, not a science (e.g., see Gage, 1978), then an explicit focus on articulating questions of practice or of student performance as a rational critical process of engaging in the inquiry cycle and bringing explicit data (either quantitative or qualitative) to the improvement of teaching is difficult to bring about. Closely related to this is the frequent concern that teachers do not have the agency or the time to effectively reflect on teaching, particularly in teams and with data that are informative to what they are doing. Too great an emphasis on testing data used to evaluate teachers and schools exacerbates the disbelief in data use for teaching, as many teachers (and researchers and policy implementers) perceive that the end of course or end of year assessments that are used for determinations of accountability do not have relevance for classroom instruction and school culture decision making. This is the tension between using more sound (assuming appropriate psychometric properties) assessments produced by state departments of education that are far removed from the classroom, or more locally and instructionally valid instruments that can inform the teaching and learning process but may not have outstanding technical quality. These summative tests fail relevancy criteria for timeliness, being removed from actual schedules of instructional decision making. In addition, they do not have sufficient grain size to examine what individual students know and can do.

Practices that suggest that annual test scores can be disaggregated by strands in the disciplines for individuals or groups of students misinform teachers about the appropriateness of data use in the classroom. The use of these summative test results is unfortunately what people often think of when assessments are mentioned, forgetting that there are many other sources of student performance data and other data that are much more informative to the instructional decision-making process. It is also part of the reason that data use has gotten a bit of a bad reputation, because it is being conflated with the overemphasis on testing and the use of wrong test results to make decisions.

## Dispositions to Think Critically About Teaching

*Thinking critically* about teaching and the relationships among classroom culture, classroom instruction, and student achievement is a broad category that is frequently mentioned when experts, professional developers, and teaching standards documents address teaching and the use of data. The research on teacher critical thinking about teaching is voluminous, but the explicit connections to critical thinking and data use are only beginning to emerge. Thinking critically suggests a more rigorous focus on data rather than anecdotes in characterizing teaching and connecting practice to student outcomes.

For instance, when a beginning teacher is required to reflect on how well a particular lesson or set of lessons was implemented, the evidence that the novice brings to bear frequently focuses on whether or not the students liked or were engaged with the activities. The teacher might touch on the extent to which the students behaved well during the lessons. However, rarely does the novice teacher have the opportunity to sit down with a mentor and reflect on the data about students that he or she used to plan the lesson or to examine specific evidence of student learning (or lack thereof) that shows how the lessons affected their knowledge and skills.

In the same way, only recently has the focus of teacher reflection in practice moved the emphasis toward the examination of specific data-rich artifacts of teaching whose association with student learning are carefully planned. When teachers engage in professional learning communities that focus on specific characteristics of students (including demographic, attendance, and behavioral data) *and* well-articulated statements of learning objectives *and* rich evidence of student performances, they have the potential to truly use data to inform instruction.

## Belief in a Continuous Inquiry Cycle for Improvement

Connected directly to the epistemic underpinnings of the inquiry cycle as a good heuristic by which to consider knowledge and skills of data literacy for teachers is a need for teachers to *believe that improvement in education requires a continuous inquiry cycle*. This goes beyond knowing what and how data are effectively used in the inquiry cycle to believing in inquiry in teaching and engaging in that inquiry on a continuous basis. Having this belief distinguishes the teacher who has taught the same lesson over and over from the teacher who consistently works to expand his or her practice.

A physical education teacher was working with a group of students, helping them improve their accuracy at the free-throw line on the basketball court. Over a week of practice, one student consistently hit more than 50% of his shots. Another student had varied performance over time. The teacher began by collecting simple statistics on percent of free-throws made and then made global analyses and interpretations about the level of success. Over time, the teacher realized that percent of shots made was too simplistic an indicator to provide diagnostic information. He then began to observe closely the techniques the students used. Did they follow through on their shots? Did they use their legs properly to gain momentum? Did they fall away from their shots? Were their hands placed properly on the ball? The collection of additional data enabled the teacher to make more precise diagnostics that then led to instructional strategies to help the two students improve their performance. The teacher and the students began collecting more data after the instructional intervention, recognizing that the process of instruction, data collection, and analysis of outcomes was an ongoing cycle of inquiry.

## Belief in Collaboration

*Believing in the value of collaboration* and having the opportunity to do so is another underpinning for data literacy for teachers. Teaching behind a closed door is also not conducive to data literacy for teachers as it is difficult for teachers in isolation to have rich data sources and the opportunity to be more objective about their instructional practices. Relying on the findings from infrequent and superficial evaluations of teaching by a supervisor or principal does not provide teachers with the opportunity to engage in a substantive examination of problems of practice associated with a particular set of learning difficulties of students.

Teachers in an elementary school meet regularly to discuss student performance. They examine data and discuss the implications for instruction. There are times that a particular teacher will raise a question of how to address specific students' learning or behavioral issues and seek advice from colleagues. Teachers who may have had the students previously weigh in and provide insights into strategies that worked in the past.

Teachers need to be able to communicate with colleagues about the data and seek help in interpreting the information and transforming them into instructional action. They must be open to input from colleagues from whom they are seeking guidance. They must be willing to admit to successes and failures, in an environment that promotes such openness through trust in the collaborative process.

## Belief in the Value of Data to Communicate to Others

A corollary of believing in the value of collaboration is a *belief that multiple stakeholders need data* that come from the classroom. For instance, parents are important consumers of data from classrooms. Frequently, the only information that parents systematically get about their child's performance is a grade. Without sufficient information about the extent to which and why a student is not doing well in the classroom, the parent is dissociated from helping the teacher address the student's learning needs. Even more important stakeholders in the use of data are students themselves. Central to one of the elements of effective data use is formative assessment in the classroom. Without an understanding of how they are progressing in their learning in a way that helps them identify what they need to do next, students are at a loss as to how to proceed.

## Disposition to Use Data Ethically

We included in our cognitive framework in Chapter 3 (Figure 3.4) a focus on teachers' understanding of and ability to apply the principles of data privacy in ways that protect students. And understanding that these principles of data privacy apply in informal settings outside of schools, such as conversations about a student with a colleague while standing in the line at a grocery store, is important (Mandinach, Parton, et al., 2015). However, teachers also need to believe in the ethical use of data on multiple levels. Beyond the appropriate understanding of the legal and regulatory requirements around data use such as FERPA and HIPAA, teachers need to believe that data should be used in the classroom in ways that will not embarrass or lower the self-esteem of students. In addition, hallway conversations between teachers should not provide information about student performances in ways that identify particular students.

The topic of the ethics and responsible use of data has become an increasingly important issue as data breaches in the public domain and in education continue to occur. As we indicated in Chapter 2, *Phi Delta Kappan* ("Privacy and school data," 2015) devoted an entire issue of the magazine to data privacy and confidentiality to raise awareness in the teaching field. Multiple organizations are seeking ways increase public awareness about the importance of the issues. The issues will continue to plague education as unsuspecting educators innocently seek technological solutions and apps that may have underlying structures that violate the principles of privacy. We all need to be aware and better educated about the challenges.

It is unclear whose responsibility it is to ensure that educators understand the fundamental principles of using data ethically and protecting the privacy and confidentiality of student data. Training educators in the ethical responsibilities of data use perhaps should be part of the onboarding

> Two teachers were chatting in the checkout line of the local super-market. They were discussing some students who were performing well and others who were struggling. They were innocently exchanging ideas on how to address some of the issues the struggling students seemed to be having. One of the teachers happened to mention two students by name as a parent walked by and overheard the conversation. The parent then called the school principal to complain that her child's right to privacy had been violated.

process by the human resources departments of school districts. It may be the responsibility of teacher preparation programs. It clearly has become an essential skill set for all educators from leaders to teachers to school data clerks.

### Dispositions Around Communication

Finally, a number of the statements around effective data use from our experts focused on the beliefs and skills in the importance of communication skills with multiple audiences. Knowledge of how to communicate about data extends across multiple aspects of the "Data Use for Teaching" framework articulated in Chapter 3 (Figure 3.4). While only one of the elements of the inquiry cycle explicitly articulates communication, the ability to present and explain all of the elements and subelements of the framework for data literacy for teachers are communication-intensive. Communication takes many forms. It can be about teachers talking to their students about student data. It can be about teachers having conversations with parents about their child's performance or behavior. It can be about teachers communicating through collaborative inquiry and data teaming processes.

Educators need to know how to talk *about* data, and they need to know how to communicate *with* data. They must know their audience and how to position the data in a way that is understandable to a parent, a student, or other educators. For example, when speaking with parents, teachers might communicate by using representative examples of performance or behavior. When providing feedback to students, teachers should communicate using concrete, constructive, and timely feedback on performance that helps the students understand the steps they need to take to improve performance. Different audiences require different communication strategies. Educators must know their audience and adapt accordingly.

# CHAPTER 5

# Improving Data Literacy Among Educators

## A Study of Four Schools of Education

This chapter provides an in-depth exploration of four schools of education in terms of how they are addressing the growing need to improve teachers' data literacy. As noted earlier, policymakers believe the use of data and evidence is an important skill that will improve practice and stimulate continuous improvement (Duncan, 2009a, 2009b, 2009c, 2009d, 2010a, 2010b, 2010c, 2011, 2012a, 2012b; Easton, 2009). Yet in a recent study Mandinach, Friedman, and Gummer (2015) found that although schools of education report they have data courses or are integrating data-related topics into existing courses, they really are conflating data literacy with assessment literacy. This chapter, based on that study, examines the content of courses and practica at four institutions to gain an understanding of how data-driven decision making is being addressed in teacher preparation curricula. It also examines the processes of implementation that institutions have developed as they make decisions about and roll out courses, curricula, and practical experiences for teacher candidates. The case studies serve as examples that are scalable as model programs.

### AN OVERVIEW OF THE SCHOOLS OF EDUCATION

To focus on the realm of possibilities for providing teachers with an effective education on data collection, use, and assessment, we investigated three innovative, urban teacher preparation programs with residency components. These programs have flexibility to take creative and cutting-edge approaches that may not be possible in traditional preparation programs. As Thorpe (2014) notes, the residency programs may provide more in-depth practical experiences, mentoring opportunities, and collaboration than traditional programs and may also provide a different structure for coursework.

We studied these programs to understand how they are able to introduce, integrate, and provide preparation around data literacy. These sites served to provide indications of what might be possible, but we recognize that scalability and generalizability to more traditional programs might be problematic. Thus we also looked at one traditional program, selected because of its reputation for having integrated data literacy into its curricula and practica, as well as having adopted a data culture within the institution. This program would provide evidence of what might be possible in more typical teacher preparation programs.

At all four schools we elicited the information we wanted through interviews with administrators, professors, institutional researchers, other relevant staff members, and current and former teacher candidates. The interviews focused on course and curricula content, and on implementation processes and historical questions. Interviewees were specifically asked about the courses and practical experiences in which data-related concepts were taught, differences between "data literacy" and "assessment literacy" concepts, the kinds of data to which teacher candidates are exposed, and the institutional culture of using data for improvement.

## HOW THE SCHOOLS INTEGRATE THE USE OF DATA IN THEIR CURRICULA

### The Possibilities for Education in Data Use

We approached the schools with the mindset that they could be termed "exemplary"—that is, exemplary in terms of a focus on integrated data literacy into their curricula and teacher candidate experiences. We examined the programs along several dimensions: (1) how data literacy is treated in the curricula, including the skills considered important; (2) whether the emphasis is on data literacy or assessment literacy; (3) how data use is integrated into practical experiences; (4) leadership and organizational vision for data-driven decision making; (5) hiring practices; and (6) institutional use of data for continuous programmatic improvement. We found many common themes across institutions, but we also noted substantial differences that led us to modify our terminology for some programs from "exemplary" to "emerging."

### The Differences Between the Residency andrTraditional Programs

We also recognized that residency programs differ structurally and philosophically from more traditional programs in some fundamental ways. Despite that fact, we wanted to learn from both traditional and residency programs so that certain practices and tenets drawn from the programs could be made generalizable to all teacher preparation programs.

Our investigation indicated that the four programs differ in their flexibility to integrate data-related concepts into courses and practica. The residency programs also differ across the three programs we studied. For example, one program has an entire strand that focuses on data use above and beyond just a focus on assessment results. It is a stand-alone course on data use with a continuum of proficiency of data literacy. The other two residency programs deal more with assessment literacy than data literacy. The traditional program is steeped in data, with a total integration of data-driven decision making in coursework and practica. Data-related concepts are integrated into all courses as well as in the practical experiences, with a theme of using data to link teaching and learning. Professors are capable of teaching about data, and their course content reflects that emphasis. In fact, having been led by two data-minded deans, new professors were hired with the data orientation in mind. Hiring practices at the schools with residency programs take on a very different model and use specific criteria that differentiate them from brick-and-mortar institutions. First and foremost, instructors must have been outstanding teachers.

The practical experiences in all four institutions are steeped in exposure to and practice with a variety of data sources. This means that teacher candidates from these innovative programs leave having been exposed to data-driven decision making in courses and practica, but with varying emphases on assessment versus data. Assessment results still loom large.

We also found that all four programs use data for organizational improvement, devoting significant effort to creating a structure for programmatic data collection that can be fed back into organizational decision making for continuous improvement. They are applying data-driven decision making in their own institutions.

### Key Data-Related Themes for All the Programs

Organizing this review of the schools—identified here as RP1, RP2, and RP3 for the residency schools, TP for the traditional—around a number of key themes, presented below is more informative than simply providing a description of the case studies.

### Institutional Components

*Leadership and Vision.* All four institutions demonstrated strong leadership and an explicit vision for their programs. The individuals who developed the residency programs are all strong leaders with an unwavering belief that their model of preparing teachers is the right thing to do. Particularly at RP2 and RP3, the creators of the institutions hold extremely strong beliefs that traditional teacher preparation is ineffective and that their model is a better method of creating great teachers. The strength of their commitment is evident and necessary as these individuals are bucking tradition and a deeply entrenched model. RP1's leadership and vision seem less radical, but no less committed to change. They also want to produce great teachers.

RP1's model appears to be more a hybrid than a complete rejection of the traditional model of teacher preparation.

All of the programs seek to develop outstanding teachers and schools that can facilitate and produce exceptional outcomes for all students. Because of RP1's affiliation with a large urban district, the program has been providing a pipeline of new and well-trained teachers into the district who will remain in the district and who can make a difference in their classrooms (Kronholz, 2012). The institution provides a 2-year master's program with the objective of holding teachers accountable for their students. The program defines successful teachers as those who demonstrate student growth, and to that end residents are required to show at least one year of growth for each of their students. The measurement underlying this vision is dependent on the collection of evidence and the connection between teaching and learning. Much like that of the other two residency programs, RP3's vision is to develop great teachers who can be placed in the country's most challenging schools. RP3 uses a combination of practical experiences and content knowledge to prepare its teachers to be effective in urban settings.

The vision for data use is less explicit than the vision for creating great teachers in all of the programs. TP is quite explicit in the use of data for organizational continuous improvement as well as for teacher candidates to exit the program being competent in their ability to use data in their practice. RP1 is similar in its dual use of data to improve programmatically as well as for teachers' skill sets. This program seeks to have teacher candidates make a habit out of using data and having data use become a regular part of their teaching repertoires. It sees teachers as "sense makers." RP2 and RP3 both have extremely strong inclinations toward institutional data use. Yet they lack the vision for how their teacher candidates should be using data.

TP has had a history of strong leaders that have been committed to the establishment, enculturation, and sustaining of a vision—to connect teaching with learning through awareness, understanding, application, and commitment. The vision also includes educational equity, cultural sensitivity, intellectual vitality, and professionalism. This vision has been sustained and nurtured through three deans, each taking it to a more explicit level. The second dean brought the vision to a new level by transforming the entire school of education, including all faculty and administrators, into a data-driven culture. New like-minded faculty were hired and others left. The institution became data-driven in all its functioning and in how faculty teach. This vision is deeply embedded and has been sustainable with a transition to a new dean who continues the tradition and vision for data use as a means by which teaching and learning are linked and through the use of work samples. Just as in all data-driven cultures, leadership is making a difference. Data are being used institutionally for continuous improvement. TP's history is clear and is being sustained by a sequence of strong and committed deans. As for the residency programs, time will tell how this plays out in two of the three programs. The other program seems committed to data literacy as it is embedded in the curricula.

*Staffing and Personnel.* A key difference can be found between, and even among, the residency programs and the traditional institution. RP2 and RP3 have strict hiring criteria, the first of which is that instructors must have demonstrated that they are outstanding K–12 classroom teachers. This means that most professors come directly from traditional and charter school districts and are steeped in practice and experience. To be clear, they are not academics in the traditional sense of the word. They do not teach theoretically; they teach from experience. They model good teaching for the teacher candidates. RP1 hires outstanding teachers, but they also have individuals on the faculty who come from an academic tradition and can provide both theory and practice. The two instructors that teach the data course were former teachers, but one also had experience at a traditional university. We therefore consider RP1 to be a hybrid with respect to faculty staffing. It is too early to determine faculty turnover and transitions in these institutions. It also is unclear how faculty are prepared to teach in the residency programs.

TP is a traditional academic institution. Faculty are expected to be both scholars and excellent teachers. All practice faculty have been outstanding K–12 classroom teachers and are expected to be outstanding professors, modeling appropriate behavior to their students. They must model and emphasize the link between good teaching and learning. Most professors at TP do scholarly work but not with the same emphasis found at research-oriented institutions. TP definitely uses research to inform its teaching and courses.

If we consider scholarship and practice to be two important dimensions of school of education faculty, RP2 and RP3 would be high on practice and low to zero on scholarship, whereas RP1 and TP would also be high, but not quite as high, on practice but somewhere in the middle in terms of scholarship.

*Sustainability Over Time.* Given the relative newness of the residency programs, sustainability is somewhat difficult to assess. One residency program, RP2, is scaling itself to several locations throughout the United States. This fact provides some indication that RP2's model is taking hold and other large districts are interested in implementing it. RP1 is embedded in one large, urban school district, and RP3 in two large school districts. Only time will tell how sustainable these institutions are, even though some are more chronologically mature than others.

In contrast, TP, which serves a primarily rural region, has sustained its vision for data use across a sequence of deans and over a number of decades. This may be due in part to the size and cohesiveness of the school of education. It also may be due to the universality of the vision—linking teaching and learning—and the underlying methodology—using work samples. This vision has been implemented, nurtured, and honed through three deanships. It is clear that the culture of data use is deeply embedded throughout the institution.

*Use of Data for Continuous Improvement.* One of the ways that schools of education can use data is for organizational improvement. This is part of what Senge (1990) refers to as the "learning organization." Data are collected and analyzed in ways that they can be fed back institutionally for continuous improvement. All four institutions have created a strong institutional research component that uses data to provide information for the purpose of continuous improvement. Lead staff members are designated to identify key metrics about which data can be collected to provide indications of what the institution is doing well and where modifications need to be made. These metrics are linked to the programs' visions and performance frameworks. Data are collected and fed back to program administrators and professors, and used to fuel discussions about continuous improvement. The notion of the feedback loop of data is found both at the institutional level and at the course level, where professors seek data about how to improve their courses. Evaluative feedback also extends to schools where teacher candidates are placed. For the residency programs, the collaborations with the districts in which their institutions are embedded are naturally occurring and fundamental structures. There is a tight feedback loop from the mentor teachers and schools back to the residency programs. The data can be used to evaluate the residents as well as the programs. A system is also in place with TP and its surrounding districts. Teacher candidates are located in these districts for not only their practical experiences but eventually for job placements. Data are fed back to TP and, by virtue of the fact that the districts continue to hire graduates from TP, data indicate a level of quality and preparedness produced by the program.

*Placement of Students and Relationships with Districts.* All four institutions have established collaborations with local districts. This is a fundamental principle of the residency programs; they are embedded in major urban districts. The relationship between the residency programs and the districts is a formalized component of the institutional structure. Teacher candidates are placed into classrooms in these districts to work with mentor teachers as apprentices or residents. They receive on-the-job training in these residencies. Graduates of the programs often work in the collaborating districts.

TP also has established relationships with neighboring school districts for practice teaching and graduate placements. However, unlike the residency programs, TP was not established solely to provide teachers to these districts. The structure appears to be less formalized, less structured, and more collaborative. The metric here might be the tightness of the coupling between the institution and the district(s). The residency programs are tightly coupled, with almost a symbiotic relationship. TP seems more loosely coupled, with more of a relationship of convenience and proximity rather than a formalized structure or contractual relationship. This could also be a product of location. The RPs are in large, urban districts, which likely require a formal agreement for any kind of association. TP is surrounded by small cities, towns, and rural schools where partnerships may be more relaxed.

*Collaborating Institutions.* All four institutions have structures in place for collaborations with districts. The three residency programs are collaborating with local districts that provide mentor teachers and venues for their residents. TP also has cooperating districts. The residency programs also have collaborations and roots in traditional schools of education with whom they continue to work in varying degrees. RP1 has collaborated with and placed a large number of students in local schools. RP2 was an outgrowth of a local traditional school of education in its city. The collaboration now is very loose. RP3 was an outgrowth of a school of education in a distant city. Yet their collaboration continues to date and is quite formal. What is interesting about RP3's collaboration is that some faculty from the traditional institution participate in and teach in the residency program, but the inverse is not true as none of the RP3 faculty teach at the traditional institution.

RP1's program includes strategic data partnerships with schools that include a part-time data analyst. The purpose of the partnerships is to customize work according to schools' needs in terms of how data are to be used. Four components are part of the strategic work: using data to guide instruction, using data to track student progress. using data to empower the community, and building data skills and expertise. The objective of the approach is to create a data culture within the schools to ensure that decisions are made based on concrete evidence.

## Curricular Components

*Course Design.* Course design differs significantly across the four institutions. Courses at RP2 and for the most part RP3 are created and scripted with prescribed content and processes by program staff. Instructors are taught how to teach the courses. This is a scripting that enables the courses to be replicated across sites, but diminishes the notion of academic freedom for instructors to create and embellish courses as they see fit. At RP2 there is no flexibility in the course design and delivery of the course materials. Courses are scaffolded so they build on preceding ones, including the data skills embedded in the courses. At RP3 there is a small amount of flexibility, but that flexibility does not seem intentional.

At RP1 there is considerable flexibility. Professors can develop their own courses as would be possible in a traditional program. However, there are also some somewhat scripted courses, which leads to a hybrid model. RP1 has a data course entitled Teacher Research: Using Data. Two instructors teach the course, which merges data concepts with instruction. The objectives of the course are to make data use a habit of mind and ensure that the residents gain a belief in all sorts of data. There is an expansive view of what data are. Additionally, RP1 strives to integrate data use into its content and pedagogy courses, but with more or less success.

At TP course design follows a typical pattern for institutions of higher education; professors create their own courses and deliver them accordingly. The exception here is the integration of the institution's vision for linking teaching and learning using the teacher work samples as a foundational element.

**Key Competencies and Supports.** It is clear from the materials produced by RP1 that data and evidence form the basis of the competencies for teachers produced in this program. The use of data and a cycle of inquiry are common themes in RP1's curricula. The program supports teachers by providing collaborative learning opportunities, courses that are relevant to skill building for continuous improvement, timely data to guide decision making, and summer grants for study for the purpose of re-energizing. In terms of data literacy, RP1 has a continuum of knowledge and skills that begins with the knowledge of assessments and assessment literacy (the term is used broadly to mean more than just a test), then moves to data collection and management, data analysis, and ultimately to applying data to inform instruction (Urban Teacher Residency United, 2014). It is clear that data literacy skills loom large in the stand-alone data course and in integration with content and methods courses. There is a focus around an inquiry cycle, with data use becoming a habit of mind.

The key competencies for RP2 include classroom culture, self and other people, student growth and achievement, teaching cycle, and content. Courses are module-based, focusing on the five key elements of effective teaching distributed across the 2-year program. The modules vary in length from an hour to a full academic year. Forty percent of the model work is conducted online. According the program's materials, instruction links pedagogical practices to particular subjects and grade levels. The student growth achievement competency is the central focus for RP2 and includes student outcomes and socioemotional development. RP2 sees student growth achievement as a venue in which data skills help the residents seek progress along a learning pathway. RP2 also is developing microcredentials for data literacy that are seen as key skill sets. Among the ten microcredentials, six of them are more aligned to assessment literacy and statistics.

RP3 uses what is called a Teacher Practice Rubric to guide teacher candidates and residents through its program. The program has identified five key competencies: the ability to create productive and nurturing classrooms; the ability to diagnose and understand their students; the ability to set goals and enact them; the ability to foster academic discussions with students; and the ability to pursue continuous improvement. RP3 has a diagnostician strand that is based on data, even though the program does not recognize diagnosis as being grounded in data literacy.

TP abides by the InTASC standards (2013a), described in Chapter 2, which include demonstrating knowledge of learner development, learning differences, learner environments, content knowledge, application of content, assessment, planning for instruction, professional learning and ethical practice, and professional learning and collaboration. These skills and knowledge are infused throughout the curricula and in clinical experience. Additionally, TP requires students to use a cycle of inquiry in which they must demonstrate their ability to state goals and objectives; prior knowledge through pre-assessments; rationales for planning instruction; lesson planning; post-assessment; reflection; and understanding the setting, the students, and the context of instruction. Students must demonstrate these skills in their required work samples and in their clinical experiences.

***Data Literacy Versus Assessment Literacy.*** It is clear that all four institutions use data for programmatic improvement. What is less clear is whether some are teaching data literacy or assessment literacy. Even if they are teaching data literacy, they may lack the understanding of the construct or are unable to articulate the difference. The distinctions are blurred and each institution differs along a continuum from assessment literacy to data literacy.

RP1 is clearly teaching about data. It explicitly deals with diverse forms of data including attendance rates, homework completion rates, disciplinary actions, course performance, reading fluency and comprehension, mastery of subject-specific skills and content, student engagement measures, and perceptions of student climate. RP1 has a stand-alone data course that is the only one we encountered among the case studies. As noted above, two professors teach the course and most definitely its focus is on data literacy. In addition, the course attempts to integrate data use in the context of the content domains. The data course appears to permeate to other courses in the institution. RP1's overseeing organization refers to a data-literate teacher continuum that ranges from assessment knowledge to assessment literacy to data collection and management to data analysis and then to enacting data-driven instruction (Urban Teachers Residency United, 2014). But their use of the term is more in line with various types of assessments. Assessments could be of student learning, of motivation and of some noncognitive or student performance variable. Here *assessment* is not meant to be synonymous solely with a summative test, a benchmark, or other tests.

RP2 definitely is teaching about assessment literacy. This is confirmed by the emphasis found in their microcredentials documents. The sole focus was student growth based on assessments. Faculty and administrators could not describe other variables of importance, other than students' grit, as something to which teachers should attend. When probed to describe data literacy, they could not do so. Their focus was solely on their student growth index. RP3 was similar to RP2 but leaned even more toward the assessment focus. Although both institutions talked about the whole child, it was clear that there was no instinctive recognition of the need to examine diverse sources of data to inform teacher practice. The lack of emphasis and explicitness about diverse data beyond assessments (i.e., tests, in these instances) was readily apparent, despite rather direct and probing questions. RP3's diagnostician strand, however, is about data literacy, although they do not recognize it as such.

Ironically, TP, where there is a clear data culture and an emphasis on data-driven decision making, does not have a stand-alone data course. TP has multiple assessment courses that really emphasize diverse sources of data and data literacy. This is the reverse from what we found when examining syllabi and what schools of education report in the national sample (Mandinach, Friedman, & Gummer, 2015). It was clear that TP approaches data literacy from an integrated perspective. The foundation of courses and practical experiences is to use all sorts of data to inform teaching and link teaching and student learning (Girod, 2002; Rosselli, Girod, & Brodsky, 2011). Graduates leave TP knowing how to use data (and assessments) to inform their practice. This philosophy is infused throughout the curricula.

### Integration of Data Use Skills with Content Knowledge and Pedagogical Content Knowledge. 

According to our original conceptual framework for data literacy for teachers shown in Figure 3.2 (Gummer & Mandinach, 2015), effective data use consists of three interacting sets of skills: content knowledge, data use for teaching, and pedagogical content knowledge. Professional development providers who specialize in data-driven decision making focus on the data skills and are able to integrate the content knowledge, but by their own admission, do not teach how to transform the data and information into actionable instructional knowledge (Mandinach & Gummer, 2011, 2013). This is why schools of education are uniquely positioned to integrate the three components of the construct. It may also be why transformational skills from data to instruction are missing from the SLDS Grants Program State Support Group's (2015) analysis of knowledge, skills, and professional behaviors.

RP1, although providing a stand-alone data course, definitely integrates the content knowledge and the data skills, and helps link them to pedagogical action. This was a component of the data course and also of other courses the institution offers. A complete integration and embedding of the three components of the construct was evident throughout TP. Data literacy skills undergird the connection between teaching and learning so that the content domain and pedagogy are informed by the data. This philosophy is explicit throughout the curricula at TP.

The connections at RP2 and RP3 are less clear, despite direct probing of faculty about how they connect content, data, and instruction. At RP2 we were told that there is a distinct content strand. Program information notes that pedagogy is separate from content. We were unable to obtain evidence that there were any connections being made to data and then to instruction. It was as if the components were distinct silos of learning and less clear how they would be manifested in practice. The one connection that was being made was between assessment data and instruction. Assessment data were to be used to inform instruction but how that link played out in terms of coursework was unclear. A similar finding was noted at RP3 as well, where the connections were even less loosely coupled.

*Learning Beyond the Classroom: Practica.* Practical experiences for all four institutions are an essential component of teacher preparation. For the residency programs, placing the teacher candidates with mentor teachers to gain classroom experience is a fundamental component of the structure of their institutions. Just like medical residencies, these programs believe that it is critical for effective teachers to be trained on site under the guidance of practicing teachers or mentors. They believe that it is premature for teacher candidates to be effective upon graduation and that the extra time for training provides the needed time to hone their skill set. This model is thoroughly consistent with statements made by Ron Thorpe (2014), the former president of the NBPTS who nevertheless has drawn distinct differences between teacher preparation and medical preparation.

Practical experiences for TP are no less important than those described in the residency programs; they just take a more constrained amount of time. As noted above, the institution uses the InTASC standards. The institution has laid out a workbook and rubric for students' clinical experiences. This document provides guidance for the teacher candidates, clinical teachers, and university supervisors over the course of the three required terms of clinical experience.

*Support Systems for Students.* All four programs excelled at providing support for their students while they were in class and during the practical or residency experiences. The foundation of the residency programs is to provide a concrete link to a mentor teacher for support and guidance. Such support was readily apparent across the three residency programs. TP also has in place concrete supports with participating districts, schools, and teachers.

## Transportability of Programmatic Impact Into Practice

We asked each institution if it was possible to distinguish their graduates from others once they were practicing teachers. The responses were somewhat surprising. In the course of the case study at TP, the dean mentioned a study conducted within the state several years ago. The study examined the impact of the teacher preparation programs as the graduates went out into the school districts. The study indicated that there were distinguishing characteristics for the first two years of practice, but after that, the context of the K–12 schools in which the graduates were functioning washed out any differences. An interview with one recent graduate further established the importance of school context. This teacher reported that there was no data culture in her school. There were no like-minded teachers or administrators. She was overwhelmed with keeping up with her daily duties, and it was hard to find time to examine data to her satisfaction. To this teacher, data-driven decision making consisted of cranking through quantitative results in a data system. When probed further, she did admit that her teaching practice was data-driven in using all sorts of data, including formative assessment process, noncognitive measures, and other data elements. It is interesting, however, that although this teacher was trained in data use, her background in the scientific process structured her thinking about what are data and what is data-driven decision making—the formal collection and analysis of *quantitative* data.

For RP2 and RP3, there is an explicit belief that what they have taught their residents permeates their practice once they have graduated. It is unclear how accurate a statement this is because of how young the programs are. It may simply be their philosophical belief that the sustainability of training occurs. It may be that the programs are too new to have substantial data to address this issue. RP1 seems to have more sustainability, especially given that it is considerably older (est. circa 2002) and more mature that RP2 (est. circa 2010) and RP3 (est. circa 2011). Many of their graduates have gone on to teach in local schools and have stayed longer than teachers from other preparation programs.

## GENERALIZABILITY OF THE DATA-RELATED PROGRAM COMPONENTS

One of the issues we faced with reviewing only a few specially selected schools was whether it was possible to generalize the findings to the greater population of schools and departments of education. For the residency programs, traditional brick-and-mortar institutions may argue that they cannot or do not seek to replicate the model of these emerging programs. For the traditional program, its moderate size may limit the scalability to much larger and much smaller institutions. Yet, they each have attributes that may be applicable to other schools with different profiles. In fact, most of the key themes described above should be generalizable. We begin with the themes most related to data-driven decision making and then describe the more general themes.

## Data-Related Themes

*Data Literacy Versus Assessment Literacy.* This theme should not be an issue. There is no question that assessment data may be the most prevalent data source for teachers, but they most certainly are not the only source of data. The easy fix here is for schools of education to change their focus from solely an assessment orientation to a more comprehensive view of data. Including data from many disparate areas, such as health, social service, attendance, attitudes, affect, context, and the like, will provide teachers with a mindset that it is essential to look at the entire landscape of data to understand a student. The philosophical shift can be accomplished in existing courses as well as in practical experiences. It will require a slight modification of focus in content and methods courses. For example, professors can talk about data and evidence, bring in data sets, and give concrete examples of how data can inform practice in a particular content domain or in methods. It also will require the mindset change to be apparent in assessment courses. Assessment courses typically focus on how to develop items and tests about student learning. They may include fundamental concepts like "reliability," "validity," and "error." The mindset shift may be more akin to the National Center for Teacher Residencies, formerly the Urban Teacher Residency United (2014) scope and sequence mentioned above: that is, that assessment is meant more broadly than performance on a measure to test student learning. Assessments can include measuring motivation, self-efficacy, attendance, behavior, and attitude.

*Stand-Alone Courses Versus Integration Across the Program.* As mentioned in Chapter 1 (see also Mandinach & Gummer, 2013b), there are challenges to and benefits from both models. Not every institution has someone who can teach a course on data-driven decision making, and in many institutions existing faculty may be unwilling or unable to include a data orientation. Of the four schools, two institutions (RP1 and TP) had stand-alone courses, and all, more or less, had some degree of integration. The concepts of data use can be found in content and methods courses as well as practical experiences, not just the stand-alone courses. Clearly, TP had completely integrated data into their curricula and practica. RP1 had a stand-alone course, but the concepts resonated throughout the program. RP2 and RP3 claimed to have integrated a data perspective, but it was less established and had a decidedly assessment orientation.

Our takeaway message is that the integration of a data orientation is essential for all institutions. Having a data course would be a helpful addition to the integrated model. Yet we recognize that for some institutions, having a stand-alone course may be impossible or impractical due to hiring constraints or size. This is why we strongly recommend that schools of education work toward a model in which existing courses and existing faculty begin to include data-driven concepts and skills.

***Data-Use Skills with Content Knowledge and Pedagogical Content Knowledge.*** As we have noted (Gummer & Mandinach, 2015; Mandinach, Friedman, & Gummer, 2015; Mandinach & Gummer, 2012), data skills require an integration with content knowledge and pedagogical content knowledge in order for them to inform instructional practice. Data skills in isolation are an abstraction. They need to be informed by teachers' knowledge of their domain, students' expected learning trajectories, and teachers' knowledge of what to do with the data within the context of the content to transform the information into actionable instructional knowledge.

Some of the programs, in particular TP's, did an outstanding job of integrating the data use for teaching skills with content knowledge and pedagogical content knowledge. The key here is making data actionable. TP does this through the vision to connect teaching and learning, with data serving as the foundation to inform that connection. Teaching about data in isolation does not provide information about how to interpret the data devoid of the context of a content domain, nor does it provide information about how to transform the information into instructional action. The takeaway message here is that in order for data use to be meaningful, the concepts and skills must be embedded within content and pedagogy.

***Bringing a Data Culture Into the School of Education.*** The themes yielded three components that can facilitate a data culture. First, it is important to make explicit that underlying the premise of teaching is the need to be evidence-based. Effective education links teaching and learning with data underlying the tight coupling to provide evidence about student and teacher performance. Second, courses in schools of education should reflect this perspective. It can be reinforced by the integration of a data orientation in courses and practical experiences. It can be further reinforced by including hands-on experiences so that teacher candidates acquire practice and facility with the examination of data. Third, schools of education should model a data orientation by developing a data culture. As a learning organization, schools of education should be using data for the purpose of continuous improvement as an institution and by professors. The four schools examined here all have such an orientation. They all have structures in place to collect, analyze, and interpret data that will allow them to identify steps toward continuous improvement. For example, RP2 has a research director who examines how their students are performing in their residency settings. These data are fed back into a program improvement cycle to determine the need for changes in how the students are prepared before they go out into the schools.

A data culture in a school of education looks very much like what was observed in TP. The dean has an explicit vision for how data can be used for programmatic improvement. That vision resonates throughout the institution. It makes clear the expectation that faculty and administrators must be informed by data. Data are used in a feedback cycle to inform decisions. There may be meetings in which faculty and staff convened to examine trends in data and discuss possible steps for improvement. Investments are made in both the human and technological infrastructures to support data use; that is, there is a provision for ensuring faculty know how to use data and that there are data systems to support the collection and analysis of data. The predilection toward data use may weigh in as a factor in faculty hiring decisions.

## General Themes

*Leadership and Vision.* All four institutions have strong leadership and a vision for data use, particularly for institutional continuous improvement. TP is an example of continued leadership that makes explicit the importance of teachers using data to link teaching and learning. This leadership has set the stage for the development of curricula, programs, and practical experiences that are grounded in data use. The vision has been sustained over administrative transitions because of the degree to which it is embedded institutionally. The three residency programs also have leadership with explicit visions, however, with less emphasis on data use as part of their programs. The take-away message here is the importance of leadership, the vision that is created, and the sustainability of that vision over time and transitions.

*Staffing.* Hiring and staffing flow from leadership. Setting aside the hiring of a faculty member who can teach a stand-alone course, it is also important to hire professors who are data oriented as opposed to those who may not embrace data. Such faculty are more likely to be willing to integrate data concepts into their course content if they understand and are comfortable with data use. It may, however, be more difficult to ask existing faculty to embrace data when it is not a typical perspective for them. Given the relatively low faculty turnover rate at most traditional schools of education, institutions should work to develop an understanding of the importance of data within their current faculty. This can be done through professional development and workshops with faculty and staff. Some teacher preparation programs are now reaching out to us and to other experts to help them implement a data orientation and culture.

The major difference in staffing noted among the schools is between TP and the residency programs. Two of the residency programs' sole criterion for hiring was that the applicants must have been outstanding teachers in K–12 settings and believe strongly in the mission of the residency program. This is not the typical hiring criterion for a professor in most schools of education, unless perhaps they are solely professors of practice. Rather than showing any potential bias against this model, it might be safe to say that to produce well-rounded educators, there must be a balance between providing fundamental knowledge of the field of education and providing excellent role models who have proven themselves as effective teachers.

*Practica.* All four institutions have strong practice teaching experiences as part of their programs. As Thorpe (2014) notes, one cannot expect a 21-year-old with no experience to walk into a classroom and immediately become an effective teacher. The process takes time, which is why the medical residency model is so attractive. Learning a trade under the guidance of mentor teachers where the teacher candidates have time to evolve and improve their skills make the residency model appealing. Perhaps it is a model that can be adapted in some way by the more traditional programs. By this we mean that practice teaching may require longer exposure than is the current model, and be done under the watchful mentorship of expert and experienced teachers who also understand the need to be data literate.

*Links to Schools and Districts.* The four institutions all have explicit and collaborative links to local school districts for the students' practical experiences as well as subsequent job placements. What stands out among them is the formalized feedback loop to the institution for both organizational improvement and student improvement. They take seriously the feedback and data they receive from participating districts in order to determine steps for improving their program as well as informing the teacher candidates about their performance.

## Conclusions About the Schools' Data Literacy Components

The findings from this examination of four schools of education indicate that even among institutions that are considered "emerging" in terms of innovative uses of data and the integration of data literacy into their programs, there is still a conflation between data literacy and assessment literacy. Clearly, some institutions focus on assessments, while either ignoring or de-emphasizing the importance of other sources of data to inform teachers and provide a comprehensive picture of the students. Even when a whole-child perspective is emphasized, representatives from the institutions are unable to articulate the difference between the two constructs, reverting to assessments as the means by which teachers understand their students. This is more than a confusion in terminology. It is a fundamental belief among many educators that assessments of student learning should be the sole source of information.

Stand-alone courses, integration, or both—that is the question. In this small sample, we have an excellent example of a stand-alone data course that integrates data skills with content areas. We also have an excellent example of the integrated approach in which data-driven decision making forms the foundation for fueling the connection between teaching and learning for course work, for practical experiences, and for organizational decision making about continuous improvement. The decision may not be *either* but *both*, depending on the context and constraints of the institution. Not every school or department of education has a faculty member who can teach a stand-alone course on data-driven decision making or data literacy. Not every institution has faculty willing to integrate a data culture throughout the curricula. What is clear, however, is that data skills cannot be used in isolation. They must be embedded within a content domain, using teachers' content knowledge to contextualize the data. The data skills in conjunction with the content knowledge then provide the needed information to allow teachers to transform the information into instructional action through their understanding of pedagogical content knowledge. The trilogy of skills interact in fundamental ways to produce teachers' data-driven instructional practice.

## IMPLICATIONS FOR SCHOOLS OF EDUCATION

Does training wash out over time because of the context of the schools where teachers end up teaching? The study that TP described (see above in "Transportability of Programmatic Impact Into Practice") may resonate across all schools of education to some degree. No matter how well teachers are trained, context can make a difference. If there are insufficient supports for new teachers, whether around data-driven decision making or any other skill set, or if the needed infrastructure does not exist, the graduates will be fighting an uphill battle to continue with the practices they have been taught. For data use, the impact might be on any one of the following: working in a data culture; having a data coach; collaborative inquiry through a data team with common planning time to discuss data; the belief in diverse data and not just test results; a focus on all students, not just "bubble kids"; a view toward a whole-child perspective; and building leadership that provides a nonevaluative, nonthreatening, and trusting environment in which data dialogues can occur.

Questions remain about the scalability of the findings and the extent to which they can be applied to diverse teacher preparation programs throughout the country, especially because we only studied one exemplary traditional institution. First, is it possible to scale the findings from residency programs to more traditional institutions? Some lessons can be drawn from the residency programs, whereas some components may not be easily translatable. Even the scalability of the findings from the one traditional institution that we studied to others may be problematic because of the diversity across schools of education. The program under examination here falls somewhere in the middle of the range of institutions; it is neither an enormous school such as Ohio State or Michigan, nor is it a two-person education department as can be found at very small institutions. It is, perhaps, a typical land-grant, state institution with its roots as a state teacher college. In that role, it provides a large number of teachers to school districts in its region.

Top education policymakers such as former Secretary Duncan, former Director of the IES John Easton, and current Director Ruth Neild see data-driven decision making as the means by which continuous improvement in schools and classrooms will occur. The U.S. Department of Education has been focusing on the development of the technological infrastructure to make data use possible at the state level (NCES, 2015a) for more than 10 years. The Department has paid less attention to building the human capacity to actually use data at the state and local levels. However, to build capacity among educators, institutions of higher education must play an essential role in preparing educators to use data, that is, to be data literate. Understanding what is possible from exemplars and understanding the implementation process by typical institutions will help the scalability of findings to other schools of education in terms of the kinds of courses, the objectives and content of those courses, plans for such courses, and the leverage points for affecting change in schools of education to include courses on data-driven decision making concepts. If courses to train educators to use data are to be incorporated into schools of education, or data concepts infused into existing courses in a scalable manner, the field needs to understand how successful implementation has occurred.

The field is coming to recognize that simply offering professional development at the inservice level is not sufficient as a comprehensive approach to preparing educators to use data. Training around data use should begin early in educators' preparation and continue through their careers. Schools of education are the venue where such learning experiences must occur if the field is to rise to Secretary Duncan's challenge for all educators to use data effectively to inform their practice. Yet it is clear that many challenges and obstacles exist and must be remediated if the goal of broad integration of data literacy in schools of education is to occur. We have provided an indication of some of the necessary structures and components to make this objective a reality.

## NOTE

We would like to acknowledge the support of the Michael & Susan Dell Foundation which provided the funds for this work. We would also like to acknowledge the collaboration with and contributions of Jeremy Friedman, Micah Sagebiel, and Ashley Craddock. A version of this chapter was presented at the 2015 annual conference of the American Educational Research Association, Chicago, IL (Mandinach & Friedman, 2015).

# CHAPTER 6

# Data Literacy in Schools of Education
## The Current Landscape

This chapter provides a fusion of the topics we have discussed in the preceding chapters by attempting to understand what is happening in schools of education in terms of data literacy within teacher preparation programs. Based on our research and work with practitioners in the field, we explore salient issues that need to be addressed and that might still require additional research. We begin by briefly reviewing findings from a survey we administered to examine what schools of education are doing to build the human capacity around data use. We then discuss issues related to preparing teachers to use data. The first issue we address is where along the developmental continuum, from teacher candidate to experienced teacher, should data literacy be introduced and reinforced, and what are the possible impacts for data literacy preparation early versus later in teachers' careers. The second and related issue concerns preservice preparation and what that might look like in the ideal. Third and also related is the adequacy of inservice training and professional development. The chapter concludes with a discussion of emerging trends, such as virtual courses, hybrids, and Massive Open Online Courses (MOOCs), as ways of doing broad-scale preparation for educators around data literacy.

### A REPRESENTATIVE SURVEY OF DATA LITERACY IN SCHOOLS OF EDUCATION

As we began to consider what it would take to prepare educators to be able to use data in schools of education, we realized that it is was important for us to be informed by data about the landscape of course offerings in teacher preparation. Anecdotes and isolated cases reported by colleagues would be insufficient. It would be both ironic and inappropriate for us to speak about the importance of data literacy and the actions that schools of education need to take without being armed with evidence about what the institutions are doing with respect to courses on how to use data. The complete study and survey results are reported in Mandinach, Friedman, and Gummer (2015) in an article in *Teachers College Record*.

## Data on the Landscape of Courses to Support Data Literacy

Thus we developed a survey to be sent to a nationally representative sample drawn from all the schools and departments of education across the country. We considered the vast variation across institutions, from huge state colleges of education, with hundreds of faculty members, to moderate size institutions, to very small departments where there may be only a few instructors. Of course, our expectations for the integration of data literacy might differ based on the characteristics of the schools of education.

The survey focused on the following questions:

- What do schools of education say they are doing in terms of course offerings?
- What really is being taught in the courses? This question was triangulated with data from a review of course syllabi submitted by some survey respondents.
- What do states require in terms of data literacy for teacher candidates? Data for this question was triangulated with the examination of state licensure documents.

We sent the survey to 808 institutions and received 208 responses (a 25.7% response rate). The responding institutions represented 47 states as well as the District of Columbia and the Virgin Islands. Over two-thirds of the institutions were public, reflecting the oversampling of the public domain. Of the institutions, 84% offer bachelor's degrees and 78% offer master's degrees. We had hoped for a higher response rate, but the survey was clearly impacted by a recent report published by the National Council on Teacher Quality (Greenberg, McKee, & Walsh, 2013). NCTQ had rated schools of education and had left negative feelings among administrators that such data collection would be used as part of a critical attack against teacher preparation programs. Our survey was viewed similarly, as having the potential to criticize schools of education unfairly, so the institutions were gun-shy.

Despite the lower-than-desired response rate, the institutions that responded had broad reach in the education community; they employed up to 10,776 full-time and 10,749 part-time faculty members, who taught as many as 96,543 preservice teacher candidates. The institutions were diverse in terms of the geographical location and size (23% enrolled more than 500 teacher candidates per year).

## An Overview of Survey Responses

One of the main questions we sought to answer was whether institutions had a stand-alone course on data use. According to administrators, there are challenges to having such a course, so it was important to determine whether such courses exist. Challenges include not having a professor qualified to teach about data, no flexibility within the curriculum, the perception that data use is not sufficiently important compared to other curricular needs, and no money to support such courses.

The survey results indicate that 62.4% of the respondents report having a stand-alone course whereas 92% report that data use concepts are integrated into other courses (e.g., teaching methods, measurement, instruction, educational psychology). Public institutions (65.7%) were more likely to have stand-alone courses than were private institutions (55.2%). Only a small difference was found for integration of data into other courses (91.3% vs. 92%).

For the stand-alone courses, the survey results indicated that such courses are:

- Required for a teaching degree (80% of the time)
- Intended for the target audience of preservice teacher candidates (84.6% of the time)
- Taught at the undergraduate level (71.6% of the time)
- Delivered in a face-to-face setting (83.8% of the time)
- Listed with a tenure track professor as the instructor of record (58.1% of the time)
- Designed to include a component in which students may access and examine authentic data from K–12 students for whom they can make educational decisions (72.4% of the time)
- Designed to include a component in which students may access and examine simulated data (78.3% of the time)

Respondents were also asked about the data-related topics addressed in both stand-alone and integrated courses. The most commonly addressed topics included concepts such as how different data are collected, data quality, and assessments (summative and diagnostic). Yet key data topics such as data systems and data dashboards were rarely addressed. Understanding the technologies that can support data use is an important skill for teachers, so teacher candidates should become familiar with the various applications and then gain a deeper knowledge specific to the tools they will encounter in their schools and districts.

To address the potential conflation of or confusion about data and assessment courses, we conducted an analysis to differentiate topics that were assessment-related versus those that were deemed not related to assessments. We gave the respondents a list of topics that were related either to data use or assessment and asked them to identify what was covered in the courses. Results from the survey indicate that assessment topics are more prominent parts of courses they consider data courses. The responding institutions' focus is clearly on assessment data instead of data more broadly defined.

The survey asked about state regulations that require teacher candidates to demonstrate data literacy. The respondents are unsure about whether their states do or do not include data literacy in their licensure and certification requirements. The survey also asked if institutions have any plans for developing a course on data and less than half the respondents (45.7%) report having such plans. Triangulating the survey results with our knowledge of state and federal requirements, apparently the emphasis on data use in the regulations has not been strong enough to stimulate change in the institutions. Clearly, if change is to happen, the institutions must want to change because they are not readily responding to state regulations or federal emphases.

Given these results, we conducted a deeper dive into a select sample of syllabi provided by 48 respondents, with the purpose of either confirming or disconfirming a suspicion that the reported courses on data were not data courses but, rather, assessment courses. Despite being very clear in the survey about what we meant by data courses, we were concerned that respondents were conflating data and assessment. This suspicion was further fueled by the many colleagues we know who teach data-driven decision making, but only for administrators, and not teachers and teacher candidates. If these colleagues, many of whom are at the forefront of the work on data use, are not teaching in teacher preparation programs, then we wondered what was really happening. We were concerned that the results overreported data courses and that the respondents conflated data with assessment courses.

The examination of the syllabi confirmed our suspicions. Indeed, the courses for which syllabi were submitted were overwhelmingly assessment courses, not data courses. There was a clear emphasis on assessment as a process and assessment data as student performances in the courses to the exclusion of other sources of data. Few courses included a comprehensive view of data sources, choosing only to focus on student performances, usually as part of an assignment on tests or quizzes as part of a lesson plan and analysis.

## An Analysis of Current Data Education Practices

We had hoped that responses to a nationally representative sample and a carefully constructed survey with precise definitions of what is meant by a data course would provide definitive answers about the extent of the education on the importance of data use received by teacher education students. However, in part because of the depressed response rate, the results provide insights and directions more than definitive findings. Certainly having 208 institutions that serve nearly 100,000 teacher candidates respond to the survey provides information about a considerable number of institutions that prepare teachers. Yet we do not know how representative of all teacher preparation programs the respondents really are. They are reflective in many respects, but we cannot know if there was a response bias from those who did respond.

What we do know from the survey is that schools of education think they are teaching about data-driven decision making, but what they are really teaching about is assessment. And this is done more through an integrated approach than through stand-alone courses. By these very facts, the conflation of data literacy and assessment literacy looms large. As we have already said, certainly assessments are a major source of data for teachers, but not the sole source. This focus limits the scope of inquiry for teachers to the more easily measured aspects of student performance, without regard to other domains that impact students, such as motivation, engagement, attendance, health, and behavior, to name a few. The focus on assessment as an objective, quantifiable data source does not help prepare teachers to consider the importance of qualitative data from teacher or student reflections of classroom experiences.

The survey did not indicate a lack of internal capacity in schools of education to teach about data, perhaps because the respondents were indeed thinking only about assessment data. We question whether at most institutions there is a faculty member who can teach a stand-alone data literacy course and if faculty members are sufficiently knowledgeable about how to integrate data concepts into existing courses.

The remainder of this chapter addresses some of our looming questions that have arisen from the survey and our related work. Each study has provided us with different perspectives on issues like when should data-driven decision making be introduced in teachers' careers, should there be stand-alone courses as well as the integrated perspective, and what are the best media to get broad-scale access to data courses.

## THE PROCESS OF DEVELOPING A TEACHER FOCUS ON DATA

When we began the work on data literacy, the question emerged about when in teachers' career it is best to introduce the concepts that surround data use. As noted in Chapter 3, many of the participants in our early expert panels felt that data literacy should start as early in teacher preparation as possible. They indicated that preservice teachers should have experiences collecting data during early observations and should have the opportunity to reflect on the quality of the data and how the data might be used to improve teaching. They further argued that each course in the teacher preparation program should include a focus on data, as this would support the candidates becoming reflective practitioners and help them recognize the empirical nature of questions about the quality of teachers.

Other participants in our early conferences felt that it was better to wait until later in the teacher preparation program or during sustained field experiences to emphasize a focus on data literacy for teaching. This position was based on the belief that it would be best to wait to address data literacy until the new teacher was out in the classroom during an induction phase or in the first years of teaching, given the complexity of using data. At the most extreme end of this continuum was the expert who felt that data literacy for teaching was an inservice topic and that it was preferable that new teachers be as close to a "blank slate" on data literacy as possible. He felt that teachers learn best about how to use data effectively to inform their teaching when they are in a collegial environment in the classroom and interacting with other teachers, such as in a data team where a focus on data can be tightly coupled with classroom practice (Mandinach & Gummer, 2012).

Teacher preparation programs are intensively laden with a plethora of topics that preparing teachers need to understand and a wide range of skills that they need to practice and refine. Stiggins and Conklin (1992) have argued for years that there is relatively little room in the preservice program for a focus on assessment literacy, and an expansion of the nature of the data and analyses that need to be addressed for a teacher to be data literate adds to the load on teacher preparation programs. However, we feel that it is important to introduce the new teaching candidate to the importance of data as information to help structure reflection as early as possible. Below we consider some ways that data can be incorporated both in the preservice teacher preparation program and inservice professional development.

**Preservice Preparation**

A focus on data literacy might start with the education foundations course that many teacher candidates take at the beginning of their preservice experiences. When preservice teachers are examining the history of education, they might be asked to reflect on the difference in demographic characteristics of students across different eras of education. Articulating who the students and teachers were in these time periods provides an introduction to the idea that data do not arise just from assessments. Educational philosophy courses could include ethical uses of data as part of their focus.

Early field experiences that require preservice teachers to interact with students on a short-term basis provide the opportunity for the practicing teachers to collect data about those students and to work with the mentoring teachers about their use of data. Questions about data privacy and the ethical use of data can be introduced at this point, providing an anchoring experience in this aspect of data literacy. In cooperation with the mentoring teachers, the preservice teachers might collect observational data that they would then discuss with the classroom teachers, supporting the notion that data to inform teaching continuously emerges during the teaching experience. This of course assumes that mentoring teachers have sufficient data literacy themselves.

Courses that focus on ethnic diversity or special needs students are full of opportunities to develop data literacy. A course that focuses on culturally appropriate teaching might start with information about the demographics of students in a typical classroom, emphasizing the importance of knowing who students are. In our examination of data literacy syllabi discussed above, it was the courses that addressed special needs students that had the greatest focus on data literacy with assignments that required the preparing teacher to collect multiple forms of data about the students and to integrate those data into profiles of students.

Methods courses also have multiple opportunities to focus on data literacy. Many of these courses include a section on assessment, and this might be expanded to include reference to multiple types of data. Assignments might include gathering demographic information about students, integrating such demographic information with previous assessment data from the classroom, and considering the role of attendance data to inform the development of lesson plans.

Technology in education courses might include an introduction to the data systems that local schools use to collect student information. Rather than just focusing on instructional technology, such as the effective choices of classroom apps or simulations, these courses could give the preservice teacher the opportunity to use data dashboards to find information about students and to examine how students are performing in the classroom. They might include a focus on behavioral management programs to examine how such systems function.

Finally, assessment courses might include an expanded focus on data from multiple sources (e.g., motivation, student performance, attitude, attendance, and behavior) rather than just tests and quizzes. Preservice teachers might have the opportunity to examine data dashboards that provide ways to interpret the sorts of inferences and conjectures about the reasons for student performances on tests and quizzes. They might be given opportunities to examine summative, end of course, or state test data and to learn about the advantages and limitations of such data sources. The technology associated with data literacy might have a prominent position in such a course.

Our own preference would be for an integrated approach to data literacy, though we see the importance of a stand-alone course for a deeper dive into some of the analytic aspects of data literacy. Both formats have challenges. Part of the problem with the stand-alone course is that we don't know much about the extent to which most professors have the experience or credentials to teach such a course. In the integrated approach, faculty have to buy into a focus on data literacy for teachers, a focus that may not have been apparent in their own experiences in the classroom. Regardless of the format of how data literacy for teaching is included in the preservice teaching experience, it is clear to us that these experiences introduce preservice candidates to using data and start them on the pathway toward full data literacy.

## Inservice Preparation and Professional Development

We strongly assert that the development of data literacy requires an ongoing effort for teachers as they move from novice to experienced educators. Until recently, efforts in data literacy for school personnel have focused on administrators who are then expected to engage teachers. In many of these cases, administrators have to make the leap from the aspects of data literacy that support their administrative practices to what will help the teacher in the classroom. Throughout this book, we have emphasized that data literacy for teachers integrates the use and the translation of data to information with teaching practices. We argue that data literacy for teachers is different than data literacy for administrators. The tight connection to instructional decision making requires as much knowledge and skill about teaching as it does about identifying, collecting, managing, and analyzing data.

Much of the inservice professional development of teachers in data literacy focuses on the use of either a turnkey model, having internal district personnel provide the training, or hiring external professional development providers. Each of these methods has challenges. A turnkey model relies on the quality of the experiences that instructors have received and the opportunity they have to implement those experiences in classroom practice before having to teach other teachers. Having internal district personnel provide professional development again relies on having sufficiently trained staff to work with individuals or groups of teachers. Bringing in external professional developers is expensive and does not support the potential to have iterative experiences of data collection, collective data analysis, and immediate connection to instructional decision making. Several of the professional development providers in our expert panels admitted that their professional development activities stopped at the classroom door, as the structure of the professional development did not permit them to engage deeply with teachers about how to connect data to instruction.

The benefits from developing data literacy for teachers are well worth the challenges that may be encountered. A significant number of school districts have made substantive commitments to helping teachers use data in their classrooms. These schools have established data teams with data team leaders who have deep knowledge of the discipline and instructional practices that they support. The schools also use data throughout different levels of decision making and emphasize the integration of multiple types and forms of data. They also invest in a significant amount of professional experiences on the data systems and dashboards that teachers are expected to use.

## EMERGING TRENDS IN EDUCATING FOR DATA LITERACY

If data literacy for teachers is to become infused into educational practice, we need new forms of professional development for teachers. They might include virtual courses such as those being designed and implemented in the Using Data Project, formerly at TERC Initiative and now known as Using Data Solutions (2014). In the course *Using Data for Meaningful Classroom Change: An Online Course*, teachers work with other teachers to identify, examine, and analyze data. Assignments require them to apply what they experience during simulations to the data they collect from their own classrooms. Course objectives include the following: why data use is important, building a foundation for the data-use process, understanding data reports, analyzing item level data, analyzing student work, root cause analysis, short-cycle planning cycles, and monitoring and adjusting instruction embedded in the formative assessment process. The online course is self-paced and intended for use by individuals or groups of educators. The Using Data Project recommends data teams take the course together.

Other courses are offered in a Massive Open Online Course (MOOC) platform. The Data Wise Project (edX, 2015) from Harvard University offers such a course. It is entitled *Introduction to Data Wise: A Collaborative Process to Improve Learning & Teaching*. The objectives of the MOOC, like the Data Wise books (Boudett, City, & Murnane, 2013; Boudett & Steele, 2007), are to build data skills and to learn how to build a collaborative inquiry process. Typically in the past, participants in Data Wise training have come to Harvard University for summer institutes to receive intensive training. The MOOC opens up the possibilities more broadly to all educators to learn about data use.

These two models have transformed more traditional face-to-face professional development into anytime, anywhere, at-any-pace learning opportunities for the current cohort of educators. It is possible for schools of education to incorporate these models into their course offerings to gain broad access to quality materials and instruction on data use and the inquiry process. The models do not require schools of education to hire dedicated faculty, but they do necessitate considerations of how and when to introduce such courses. It is possible that Using Data and Data Wise are both more appropriate for graduate level and continuing education courses. It is also possible that components of the courses may be adaptable for preservice teacher preparation. Given the newness of the two courses, a closer examination of the format and content is needed.

Finally, we consider a model that has been under discussion at WestEd with strategic partners. We have been discussing the need for what we call modular materials, that is, materials that can be integrated into existing courses in pieces that are relevant to the particular topic. The materials would be a combination of more traditional print resources, but also capitalize on various electronic media for more anytime, anywhere materials. The electronic resources might be online materials, video clips, or apps that are accessible via mobile devices. The objective is to make the materials and resources as readily accessible, easily usable, and flexible in their use as possible. Combined, the materials could be a stand-alone course. Taken separately, the components or modules could be inserted into courses. They could be used for professional development purposes or for educator self-education, if individuals had an interest in or curiosity about a particular data-related topic, such as how to protect student privacy or how to understand patterns and trends.

We endorse any or all models that provide a broad-based knowledge of data-driven decision making in education and help improve educators' data literacy. Making courses available is a critical step. Another step is making a variety of resources available, as we have done on the Data For Decisions Initiative at WestEd's website (WestEd, 2015). Helping schools of education use these resources, adopt and integrate them into their curricula, and attain broad usage are the ultimate objectives. There is much work still to be accomplished.

# CHAPTER 7

# Establishing Data Literacy for Teachers

## A Systemic Approach

This chapter is intended as a challenge to schools of education to begin to incorporate data literacy for teachers into their curricula. After two chapters of examining in some detail the existing state of data literacy in schools of education, we now explore the interactions among organizations that can influence how schools of education prepare teachers to become data literate. We believe that it is contingent upon institutions of higher education to step up to the plate and help prepare teacher candidates and current teachers to be data literate. Teacher candidates, especially, must learn how to use data effectively and responsibly so they can hit the ground running once they are practicing teachers. It is no longer acceptable or prudent for the field of education to wait until teachers are minted and in the classroom for them to acquire data literacy skills. They cannot graduate as a tabula rasa and expect the schools and districts to provide adequate training on how to use data. Training must be an ongoing part of educators' professional careers through continuous learning that begins when they are candidates and continues throughout the years of practice as teachers and possibly administrators.

We recognize that institutions of higher education function within a complex system and not in isolation. Thus this chapter explores the organizations and agencies that are key players in that system with respect to their roles and responsibilities in enhancing educator preparation. The chapter also explains the key levers for change, that is, how schools of education come to recognize the importance of data literacy and begin to integrate it into their curricula and practica. Change does not come easily, so we will also discuss the many challenges to making the reform happen.

### TAKING A SYSTEMS APPROACH TOWARD BUILDING DATA LITERACY IN EDUCATORS

Systems thinking helps organizations understand the interrelationships among components in complex systems. It serves an integrative function to address a complex problem such as the building of data literacy in educators. With systems thinking, organizations examine the structure or the interrelationships among components—the "whole of their entities"—that influence behavior over time. System thinking recognizes the hierarchical nature of phenomena and operations within multiple levels, such as schools within districts within states (Mandinach, Rivas, et al., 2006; Senge, 1990; Senge et al., 2000; Williams & Hummelbrunner, 2011). Senge's framework examines complete organizations with respect to change and looks at the complexity of interactions among system components, identifying underlying structures and causes of change. A systems approach helps organizations identify leverage points and determine where and when actions can be taken to affect change. Systems thinking also relies on the systematic collection and analysis of data for self-reflection and considers the consequences of decisions.

## KEY STAKEHOLDER GROUPS IN IMPROVING DATA LITERACY FOR TEACHERS

In order to characterize the systemic nature of improving the use of data by educators, one must characterize the key stakeholders in the system. Figure 7.1 depicts the relationships among many of the key components that influence teacher preparation. Our articulation of the stakeholders and their roles and responsibilities arose from the convening of researchers, deans, and accreditation experts (Mandinach & Gummer, 2012, 2013a). The attendees reflect the landscape outlined in Chapter 2, that is, the many organizations that are essential components in affecting change to include data literacy in teacher preparation programs. The objective of this Spencer Foundation-funded meeting was for stakeholders to discuss issues around the way that data-infused courses could be implemented in schools of education. The challenges were explored and the opportunities discussed.

### Schools of Education

Schools of education are central in improving educator data literacy by integrating data-focused courses or concepts into educator preparation programs. We envision an enhanced role for schools of education, introducing data literacy early and affirming its importance throughout an educator's career to support the enculturation of data use.

The outcome of the meeting left us with a number of unanswered questions and issues. Two questions loomed particularly large and we explored them in the previous chapter. First, when is it best to introduce data literacy to a teacher or teacher candidate? No research existed to address this question, only best guesses from the experts at the Spencer meeting and

**Figure 7.1. A Systems Map of Key Components in Data Literacy in Teacher
    Preparation**

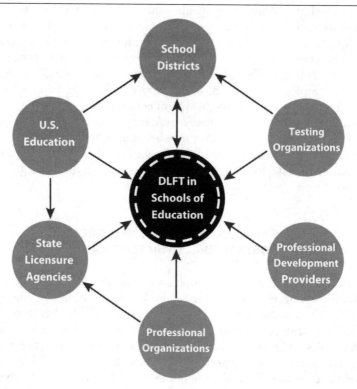

subsequently at a meeting funded by the Gates Foundation in the following year (Mandinach & Gummer, 2012, 2013a).

Second, should data literacy be introduced into schools of education through stand-alone courses or through an integrated perspective in which content and methods courses as well as practical or clinical experiences would contain components of data use? Again, at that time, there was no research and certainly no easy answers. We wondered if it made sense to have both a stand-alone course and integration throughout the curricula, or only one option. Practically, both solutions are complicated and require a systemic approach. A stand-alone course requires that there is a faculty member sufficiently knowledgeable to teach that course. In our experience and that of other experts in the field, there are few professors prepared to teach such a course. Those who do teach about data-driven decision making, do so in leadership programs, not in teacher preparation programs. The philosophy is to train leaders first, who then train the teachers. In addition, schools of education may not be able to or choose to devote a hiring slot to someone who can teach such courses. Lastly, there may be no wiggle room in the curriculum for a stand-alone course, as one dean reported to us.

The decision to develop a stand-alone course is complicated, as noted previously, but so is the decision to integrate data literacy into other courses. Integration requires buy-in from existing faculty. It assumes that these professors can integrate data into content, methods, and practica. Such full integration requires professors to rethink and retool existing courses, a task that they may resist because they are not qualified or willing to do so. After all, institutions of higher education are a bastion of academic freedom. However, as was described in Chapter 5, at least one traditional teacher preparation program has successfully integrated data-driven decision making throughout its courses and clinical experiences. This institution is a fairly typical small university with its roots as a "normal school" (i.e., an institution that trains teachers), focusing on the preparation of teachers for the local area. We acknowledge that there are many challenges, but it can be done.

Further and after much consideration, we have come out on the side of integrating data literacy as the preferred structure for teacher preparation courses. The reason for this can be found, in part, in the conceptual framework with the original three interacting domains of data use skills, content knowledge, and pedagogical content knowledge as depicted in Figure 3.2 and then in the expanded framework depicted in Figure 3.3. Our original consideration of only two of the Shulman (1987) areas of teacher knowledge comes from Edith Gummer's focus in assessment practices of teachers of science and mathematics (Gummer & Champagne, 2004; Gummer, Cohen, Gates, & Fantz, 2010; Gummer & Shepardson, 2001a, 2001b). The key component of assessment practices for teachers is a strong knowledge of the content area so that they can elicit and recognize the ways in which students demonstrate their understanding of what is being taught. In order to be able to engage the students in formative assessment practices—those that focus on not only identifying where students are in their learning, but also on what students need to experience to improve their understanding—teachers need to know how to connect their sophisticated understanding of the content with the representations of the content in teaching materials: *pedagogical content knowledge*. But this is a simplistic way to consider how data inform teaching at multiple levels.

At the heart of both formative assessment and data literacy for teachers is the *teacher knowledge and skills of learners and their characteristics*. Without an understanding informed by the learning sciences of how students think and act, the teacher is at a disadvantage in determining how to structure learning experience. While much of this knowledge and skill area might also be associated with pedagogical content knowledge, there is a much richer set of data that can inform a teacher's knowledge of learners and their characteristics. These data include demographic, behavior, and attendance data. Understanding the ways in which to use these data to support the preservice teacher to best inform classroom practices could start in early foundation courses in a teacher education program. Faculty in an education philosophy course could incorporate historical and current demographic data to support the rationale for different education programs over time. Rather than just focusing on the findings from studies in introductory educational psychology courses for teachers, faculty might provide data sets and provide preservice teachers with the opportunity to interpret the data and draw inferences. Such a course might also include exercises that focus preservice teachers on interpretations of attendance or behavioral data in scenarios that address key themes that are typically addressed in such courses. Data that preservice teachers might address could also include teacher comments and student self-reflections to provide a broader perspective of what counts as data.

*Knowledge of educational contexts* is key to understanding how to act in schools and districts. Data at the school and district level can be incorporated into educational foundation courses to help preservice teachers with experiences of what they will encounter when they start to teach. Such courses might provide opportunities for students to delve into data sites such as individual school and district report cards to help them characterize the educational settings that surround them. They might also engage in experiences with aggregated state data sets that are available at the state level, such as *EdWise* currently being developed by the Ewing Marion Kauffman Foundation (2015) so that they can situate their developing understanding of the schools and districts with which they work locally. *Knowledge of education ends, purposes, and values* are key to understanding from where the current focus on educational standards and tests has emerged. The data in the standards is not numerical, but the statements of what students need to know and be able to do that make up the Common Core State Standards in English Language Arts and Mathematics (Common Core State Standards Initiative, 2010, 2015b) and the Next Generation Science Standards (NGSS Lead States, 2013) are at the heart of how teachers use data in the classroom to determine how well students are attaining educational goals and objectives. Without the roadmaps that are illuminated by the standards, teachers' use of diagnostic and monitoring data are disconnected from instructional decision making.

We strongly considered leaving out general pedagogical knowledge and curriculum knowledge from our framework. Yet we asked ourselves how a teacher could use data to inform instruction without knowledge of what curriculum is being used and how that curriculum relates to others. In addition, the data literacy for teachers inquiry cycle is focused on teaching, and the latter half of the inquiry cycle is heavily weighted on instructional decision making. Without a focus on the decisions of data-driven decision making, teacher data use happens in a vacuum. However, one of our considerations is that much of the research on professional development of teacher data use training focuses on general pedagogical strategies that make suggestions of alternative experiences for students not well connected to the content that students are to learn. Building experiences for preservice teachers in pedagogy and methods courses that provide examples of multiple forms of data use are easy to consider. As students are learning about the principles of curriculum development, they should also be learning about implementation, and the data they generate in such exercises provide another opportunity to develop data literacy.

Additionally, as we have noted, professional development providers can focus on the data skills and they can embed them to some degree in content. But where they fall short is with the connection to pedagogy. Schools of education are uniquely positioned to integrate the three domains to address the "What do I do now that I have the data?" question. Transforming the data within the context of the content into instructional action is something teacher preparation programs should and must be able to address.

## State Education Agencies and State Licensure Agencies

Teacher preparation programs pay attention to state licensure and certification requirements. Therefore, states and their credentialing agencies can have a major impact on the introduction of courses on data-driven decision making if they expand and make explicit requirements that schools of education prepare educators on data use. Schools of education will have to respond to such requirements in state licensing and accreditation rules. According to a self-report survey of state data directors, results indicate that 13 of 47 states (four did not respond) have requirements for superintendents to demonstrate data skills in the certification or licensure process, 18 for principals, and 22 for teachers (DQC, 2014b). Progress is occurring, inasmuch as only 2 years earlier, the results indicated that 10 states had requirements for data training for superintendents, 13 for principals, and 14 for teachers (DQC, 2011, 2012). Only 11 states required data literacy as a part of the preservice credential/licensure process.

Our research (Mandinach, Friedman, & Gummer, 2015) examined the licensure documents to see what skills and knowledge that pertain to data-driven decision making states are asking of teacher candidates. As noted previously, we found that 20 states do not mention data in their documentation. Only 8 states have a data standard. Less than half the states (23) make explicit reference to skills that would be regarded as data literacy. In contrast, 37 states explicitly make reference to assessment literacy skills. Some states provide highly specific descriptions of the requisite skills, whereas others barely mention specific skills or knowledge. Some states (7) have outlined developmental continua that document what a novice data user might look like compared to more experienced data users. The seven states (AR, AZ, DE, NV, ND, OR, and SC) that have adopted the InTASC standards (2011, 2013a) are steeped in data-relevant skills.

A caveat applies here. Just because there is a requirement or because the licensure documents include data skills, there is no guarantee that schools of education are paying attention. There must be some level of accountability for schools of education to take action. One source of accountability may be the evaluations that are being leveled on schools of education to produce more effective teachers. If data literacy becomes part of the expected skill set, then schools of education may be forced to respond by including data-driven decision making as part of their teacher preparation programs. Ideally, one would hope the institutions would not need the accountability pressure to come to the same decision.

## School Districts

Another stakeholder in the teacher preparation system and the efforts to improve educator data literacy is the school district, its schools, and the practitioners actually carrying out the requirements of data use. Districts are expected to collect, analyze, and use data at all levels from central administration down to the classroom level and apply those data to inform practice and decisions. Districts employ educators who may lack the skills and knowledge around data use, but who must acquire the capacity to use data. Districts often seek help from professional development providers for training or rely on internal staff to provide inservice workshops. Such training opportunities may not be sufficient in terms of quality and substance. They may also be too little, too late in educators' careers. Districts, therefore, may seek help from schools of education because they lack the resources or the internal capacity to implement broad-scale training on data-driven decision making. Districts look to schools of education for courses for their current staff. They can also look to the schools of education to produce new teachers who have data skills and show competence in data use (Mandinach & Gummer, 2011; Mandinach & Gummer, 2012). Some districts require candidates for positions to demonstrate data literacy as a requirement of the hiring process (Long et al., 2008).

School districts often have relationships with schools of education to help prepare their teacher candidates. The candidates engage in their practical or clinical experiences under the watchful guidance of mentor teachers. Graduates accept positions in the districts. Current teachers return to take additional courses for graduate credit. It is important for districts to recognize that teachers and administrators in their districts should be able to demonstrate a level of data literacy and that these educators ideally have received their initial data literacy training in the preparation programs and have had those skills reinforced with additional professional development opportunities and the enculturation of data use within their schools. As noted in the previous two chapters, the context of schools and districts make a big difference. If strategies and ideas are not reinforced in practice, they can be washed out within 2 years after graduation. Data-driven decision making may well be one of those ideas that requires enculturation and support in schools. Having like-minded colleagues, a data team, a data coach, and supportive leadership all help support new teachers who have had data training in their preparation programs.

## Professional Development Providers

Experts in professional development, such as the Using Data Project (2015) and Data Wise (EdX, 2015), comprise another stakeholder group with a history of working with practicing educators to help them develop understandings of data-driven practice. Schools of education can learn from the professional development providers about how to develop courses on the topic or how to integrate data-driven concepts into existing courses. Schools of education could even look to the professional development providers as a resource in teaching courses, including face-to-face courses, virtual courses, or courses for continuing education credits. Schools of education then do not have to hire additional faculty or allot a faculty position to someone who knows data. Professional developers can broaden their range of influence. For example, the Using Data Project (2015) has developed an online data course. Data Wise (2015) has created a MOOC, in addition to a course offered at the Harvard Graduate School of Education. Most importantly, more educators, both at the preservice and inservice levels, will be introduced to data-driven practices and become data literate.

## Professional Organizations

Other organizations that focus on teachers and teacher preparation have critical roles in helping establish data-driven decision making in educator preparation, driving the need for more systematic preparation in data literacy for educators with accreditation and licensing regulations. Professional organizations such as the National Board for Professional Teaching Standards, the Council for the Accreditation of Educator Preparation, and the American Association of Colleges for Teacher Education can provide an impetus for creating change, explicitly emphasizing data literacy in standards and evidence for accreditation. Recall NCATE's (2010) recommendations described in Chapter 2. Their Blue Ribbon Panel states that teacher candidates "need to have opportunities to reflect upon and think about what they do, how they make decisions, and how they 'theorize' their work, and how they integrate their content knowledge and pedagogical knowledge into what they do" (p. 9). The report further states that teacher preparation must provide "the opportunity to make decisions and to develop skills to analyze student needs and adjust practices using student performance data while receiving continuous monitoring and feedback from mentors" (p. 10). These are the principles of data-driven decision making and continuous improvement applied to teacher preparation and to practice.

The Council of Chief State School Officers has a wide range of activities, some of which can target the importance of the use of data and training educators to use data. CCSSO convenes meetings of top educational officials who can influence change in their states by initiating discussions that may lead to the inclusion of data literacy among licensure and certification requirements. Consortia supported by CCSSO can include among their standards more explicit references to data literacy skills as they apply to the professions. The challenge is making the standards operational. InTASC (2011, 2013a), described in Chapter 2, has created standards for teachers. To date, seven states have invoked these standards with others considering them as their requirements. The InTASC standards are comprised of 10 specific standards: learner development, learning differences, learning environments, content knowledge, application of content, assessment, planning for instruction, instructional strategies, professional learning and ethical practice, and leadership and collaboration. Performances, essential knowledge, and critical dispositions are outlined within each standard. Data use is seen as a cross-cutting skill from which nearly 50 specific skills and knowledge could be identified as part of data literacy.

**Testing Organizations.** Teacher preparation programs pay attention to the content on national teacher licensure examinations. Testing organizations can integrate data-driven concepts into their assessments for teachers and administrators at the behest of state licensing agencies. If the assessments are a required part of the credentialing or licensure process, then schools of education are likely to respond by ensuring their students are prepared for the examinations. This is a major accountability medium.

Educational Testing Service has developed tests for educators. Currently, data-driven decision making is not part of the Praxis test for teachers, but it is included in the *School Leaders Licensure Assessment* for administrators. The latter requires data-driven decision making through the analysis of different sources of data and information to form a decision (ETS, 2005). However, we know that ETS is planning to include data literacy in revisions of their testing programs. Another test has recently been developed to measure the skills teachers need to use in their classrooms. The edTPA is a performance-based assessment produced by SCALE (2013), in collaboration with AACTE. The edTPA has a major assessment component, but data use also can be found in the test.

We suspect that if data-driven decision making is included on tests for teachers and administrators such as PRAXIS and the edTPA, schools of education will be forced to respond by teaching to the test. Testing companies will build such assessments if professional organizations and states require such skills and knowledge.

**U.S. Department of Education (ED).** Finally, the federal government can play more of a role in emphasizing the need for data literacy beyond the speeches government officials have made. Of course the mandate to improve teacher preparation programs will have an indirect effect, but only if there is a stipulation that graduates must be data literate. To date, there is neither a federal mandate nor specific funding programs to stimulate the training of educators. Although substantial funds have been devoted to the development of the technological infrastructure to support data-driven decision making, no monies have been similarly devoted to building the capacity of educators to use data to improve teaching and learning. The accountability lever is one way to stimulate action, albeit a heavy-handed one.

## WHAT CHANGES ARE NEEDED TO INCREASE THE CAPACITY FOR EFFECTIVE DATA LITERACY

### Research and Discourse to Strengthen Data Use

Our systemic view of creating data-literate educators rests on three fundamental premises. First, data-driven decision making must become part of an educator's preparation. Educators must receive systematic training in how to use data, preferably beginning in their preservice years, but continuing throughout their careers. Second, schools of education are the appropriate venue in which the needed educational experiences must first occur. They must find ways to integrate data-driven practices and principles into the training of educators. Finally, schools of education do not function in isolation, but instead in a complex system where change comes slowly. We have discussed the roles of many of the key players we see as creating an environment for change. They all must play their parts. As depicted in Figure 7.1, the players include state education agencies and their licensure components, school districts, the U.S. Department of Education, professional organizations, testing organizations, professional development providers, and schools of education.

Aimee Guidera (2013, 2014), president of the Data Quality Campaign, uses a metaphor contrasting a hammer and a flashlight to advocate for effective data use. The hammer represents accountability. If teachers do not become data literate and schools of education do not help prepare effective educators who know how to use data and can demonstrate those skills, the hammer of accountability will come slamming down. This accountability will be delivered through teacher examinations and licensing processes and evaluations of schools of education. In contrast, the flashlight represents the path toward enlightened practice, in this case the demonstration of data literacy skills that can positively impact teachers' practice. Would it not be easier for schools of education to begin to adapt data literacy before the hammer of accountability comes crashing down on them?

It is reasonable that schools of education must be the driving force for improving data literacy as the preservice preparation period is a major opportunity for the development of knowledge and skills. However, the introduction of a data-use focus into programs or courses may not be simple. It is unclear if there is sufficient motivation or perceived needs on the part of schools of education. It is unclear whether current faculty members are themselves sufficiently data literate to be able to teach such courses. A related issue is whether or not deans of schools of education believe that having a faculty slot devoted to data-driven decision making is important. This is an issue of perceived need as well as prioritization. Other priorities and pressing institutional needs may trump such appointments (Mandinach & Gummer, 2011).

From our research, we are closer to understanding how and when the concepts of data literacy can and should be integrated into teacher preparation—whether in stand-alone courses or integrated within existing courses. As noted above, integration is essential but having a data course in addition to the integration would be ideal. Data use should also be integrated into practica so that candidates can gain experience working with authentic data. This means that cooperating schools and mentors must also understand data and provide the necessary supports. Most institutions report having a data course or having integrated data concepts into existing courses and practical experiences (Mandinach, Friedman, & Gummer,, 2015), yet what really is being taught is assessment literacy rather than data literacy. The conflation of the two constructs is problematic and needs to be addressed in licensure requirements and school of education curricula. We raised the question about when is the right time to integrate data-driven decision making. It is probably safe to say that the answer is: as early as possible in the teacher preparation curricula and then reinforced throughout the program and into practice after graduation.

Our recommendations for stimulating progress in the field focus on three areas of need. First, there is a need for research to address the gaps in the scientific knowledge base to help us understand the changes that need to occur in educational practice. Second, policymakers and relevant stakeholders need to come together to discuss and work out the action steps necessary to ensure that educators know how to use data to inform their practice. Recognition and policy change do not always translate into action, which leads to the third recommendation. Stakeholders need to recognize that data are more than just assessments and that data literacy is more inclusive than and different from assessment literacy. Even forward-thinking organizations still tend to adopt the view that assessments are the only data and therefore assessment literacy is the desired skill set. The National Board for Professional Teaching Standards is one such organization that chose to take the traditional path instead of making cutting-edge statements about the need for data literacy more inclusively considered. Teachers need to know how to examine assessment data. Teachers need to know how to interpret assessment data. But teachers use more data sources than just assessment results. That recognition would dispel the overemphasis on testing.

## Research Needs

*Research on the Impact of Data Use.* A critical gap in the field's knowledge base is whether the use of data changes classroom practice and ultimately student performance. Two studies (Carlson et al., 2011; Konstantopoulos et al., 2013) found the impact of data use yielded mixed results for mathematics and reading achievement and for different grade levels. But the field still needs to more clearly understand what impact there might be at the student and teacher levels as well, including the intended and unintended consequences. By this we mean that there is an implied assumption being made that data use changes teachers' classroom practice in a positive way, and therefore impacts student achievement. We first need to explore more specifically what changes occur for teachers in their classrooms, and then find out what impact those changes have on student performance as well as on noncognitive variables, such as motivation, self-efficacy, and attitude. We also need to understand more about the mixed results; that is, why positive impacts were found for some grade levels and content areas and not in others. Exploring some of the possible explanations would be helpful, such as whether the student outcome measures were sufficiently sensitive to the intended rationale for data use or whether the implementation of the data-use practices were done with fidelity.

*Research on Policy.* Several policy-oriented issues should be addressed and better understood. First and foremost, there needs to be an alignment between what districts, schools, and educators actually do and need to do, and the actions that schools of education might take, to integrate data-driven practices into educator preparation programs. It would be irresponsible to make changes without consulting the ultimate stakeholders and end users—local education agencies. Schools of education should be responsive to those needs, whether adapting their course offerings or providing outreach through continuing education opportunities.

There is a need to explore the role that states can play in setting future policy and developing and mandating licensure and certification requirements for all educators, and to address the following questions: Can and will states require that educator preparation programs offer training on data use? Will schools of education be held accountable for their graduates to show evidence of data literacy? Can and will testing organizations introduce components of assessments that measure data use and data literacy? Will such requirements stimulate change throughout the education system and impact practice?

Research should address the role the federal government might play beyond making public policy statements about the need for educators to be data literate. A policy analysis might address whether there are provisions that can be designed for helping train the current cohort of educators and what the U.S. Department of Education can do. We know that then Secretary Duncan announced plans to improve teacher preparation (Teacher Preparation Issues, 2014; U.S. Department of Education, 2014; White House, 2014). Why not include data literacy? A parallel policy analysis might also address the roles that states can play.

***Research on Developmental Needs of Educators.*** We still do not understand the differing needs of diverse groups of educators in terms of preparation for data-driven practice. Research is needed to understand data literacy preparation needs of teachers as opposed to administrators and of novices as opposed to experts. We don't know how much is enough data literacy; that is, what is the basic minimum level of competency that should be expected of all educators. We do, however, have a better sense of what an expert looks like. Do all educators need to be experts? The answer is, probably not. Some might be consumers of information. Some might be true data nerds. Others might just need a passable level of understanding. Educators' needs will differ and the field can benefit from understanding those differences and how best to provide education and training on data literacy to address the diversity.

## A Strengthening of the Discourse Around Educator Preparation

This chapter has discussed the complexity of infusing data practices into the preparation of educators. The research we recommend above is a necessary but insufficient component of improving data literacy. What also is needed is high-level support from policymakers and relevant stakeholders beyond just the rhetoric. It is becoming clearer where and how data-driven courses can and should be integrated into course work. But the diversity of needs across preservice to inservice, and teachers to administrators, must be considered.

Continued discussion among the relevant agencies can help address some of the questions and issues we have identified. Take, for example, a sample of events from the DQC (2014a, 2014c, 2014d; Guidera, 2014; Mandinach, Kahl, et al., 2014) and a subsequent white paper on what it means to be a data-literate teacher (DQC, 2014c) that were described in Chapter 2. Particularly important is the national event *Empowering Teachers with Data: Policies and Practices to Promote Educator Data Literacy* that brought together diverse panels of experts to discuss teacher data literacy (DQC, 2014a). Included among the speakers were a chief state school officer, the president of a national organization for teacher preparation, legislative policymakers, representatives of national teacher organizations, a practicing teacher, policymakers, and a researcher. The objective was to discuss what needs to be done to ensure that the teacher workforce is data literate. The recognition of importance was clear. What was not as clear was a path that outlines action steps toward change, particularly from the national teacher organizations and school of education representatives. The white paper on teachers' data literacy was produced for the event by a panel of diverse experts from relevant organizations and agencies (DQC, 2014c). A second event on data literacy, *What's the Difference Between Assessment Literacy and Data Literacy?,* was convened on July 21, 2014 (DQC, 2014d). This event explored the differences and commonalities between the two constructs, with the objective of impressing upon the audience that assessment literacy is actually a component of data literacy and that educators need to think broadly about diverse sources of data, not just assessments. These events brought to national attention the importance of educators knowing how to use data effectively and responsibly, beyond just assessment data. More efforts like these need to be convened to dispel the notion that data and assessments are synonymous, otherwise the field will continue to conflate the two constructs.

It is our belief that change will not happen if each agency functions in isolation without a more comprehensive approach to the issue. It is also our belief that unless educators and other stakeholders begin to think of data as broadly defined as possible, the field will continue to equate data with test results, a serious constraining factor. The meeting that we convened in 2011 (Mandinach & Gummer, 2011) brought together some but not all necessary participant groups. A second meeting convened a year later included experts in the fields of data, formative assessment, research, and professional development (Mandinach & Gummer, 2012, 2013b). The DQC events have included yet other stakeholders. Their working group on data literacy had broad representation across professional organizations. However, what is needed is a more comprehensive and higher-level meeting where officials from federal and state education agencies, the professional education organizations, deans of schools of education, credentialing organizations, and other interested parties come together not just to discuss what needs to be done to affect change, but to actually map out policy changes that will necessitate and create the change that is needed.

Data-driven decision making requires that data have utility and are actionable. *Actionable* is the key term here. Bringing together stakeholders who can make action happen may be an effective means by which progress can begin to occur. Ideally, this action will occur with the flashlight in mind rather than moving just in front of the accountability hammer. The development of a systemic, comprehensive, and strategic plan is needed. If the field is left to a piecemeal approach to action, nothing is going to happen, and little, if any, progress will be realized. This issue requires buy-in from many stakeholder groups, at different levels and from varied organizations. Obtaining that agreement requires leveraging the appropriate sources of influence. It will not be easy because of the interdependencies and complexities, but it is possible.

**NOTE**

This chapter is based on an article, "A Systemic View of Implementing Data Literacy in Educator Preparation," that appeared in 2013 in the *Educational Researcher* (Mandinach & Gummer, 2013a). It also is based on a conference of experts convened in 2011 and funded by the Spencer Foundation.

# CHAPTER 8

# Helping Schools of Education Adopt Data Literacy for Teachers

This final chapter builds on our discussion of the systemic nature of the change process in teacher preparation programs described in Chapter 7. In this chapter, we examine the pedagogical implications of data literacy, explicating what data literacy looks like in classrooms and educational practice. We also examine the potential next steps that could be taken by various stakeholder groups to ensure that data literacy becomes a widespread reality. As we noted in the previous chapter, diverse stakeholder groups all play a role in the acceptance and development of data literacy, not just for teachers but for all educators. Change will not occur in isolation nor will it be easy.

## THE PEDAGOGICAL IMPLICATIONS OF DATA USE

Understanding the pedagogical implications for the "data literacy for teachers" construct requires us to think deeply about each of the domains and the components of the inquiry laid out in Chapters 3 and 4 (see Figure 3.3). The seven domains (content knowledge; general pedagogical knowledge; curriculum knowledge; pedagogical content knowledge; knowledge of learners and their characteristics; knowledge of educational contexts; and knowledge of educational ends, purposes, and values) are essential, not just to data literacy for teachers, but to teaching more generally. The five components of the "Data Use for Teaching" domain (Identify Problems and Frame Questions, Use Data, Transform Data Into Information, Transform Information Into Decisions, and Evaluate Outcomes) are the keys to effective data use. More importantly, it requires us to consider each of the skills, knowledge, and dispositions that have been identified as part of data literacy for teachers.

The interactions among the three domains are complex. Questions remain about what the developmental continuum of data literacy looks like from novice to expert and what the lowest level of required literacy necessary to use data effectively and responsibly is. Yet the "Data Use for Teaching" domain does not function in isolation; teachers need content knowledge and pedagogical content knowledge. What happens if they know how to use data but don't have a sufficient knowledge of their domain into which that data can be contextualized? Or what happens if they understand the data and their place in a learning trajectory, but lack the pedagogical content knowledge to transform the information into an actionable instructional decision?

Here are examples of two teachers who may know about data, but lack content knowledge or pedagogical content knowledge:

Teacher 1 is a high school math teacher. He is trying to determine why a group of students is struggling in math. He has looked at the results from some classroom assignments, quizzes, and answers to questions students have been given in class. He knows which students are struggling. But he is having trouble placing the specific misconceptions within the learning progression around quadratic equations. He can't readily determine his students' foundational knowledge to figure out why the students do not understand the equations. This is a case where the teacher may not have a deep enough knowledge of the domain in which he is teaching.

Teacher 2 is a fairly new middle school social studies teacher. She is struggling to help her students understand some of the similarities across historical events so that they can learn about causes and effects. She is getting frustrated with the students' failure to understand the consequences of behavior. She simply does not know what to do instructionally. The teacher seeks advice from a more experienced colleague about how to reach the students through some creative instructional experiences. This is an instance where the teacher understands the data and the content domain, but is lacking knowledge of what to do pedagogically.

In terms of the specific data use for teaching skills discussed in Chapter 3, if we walked into a classroom, would we be able to observe the skills in action? Are some of the skills more amenable to observation during data teaming rather than in classroom practice? Are some of the skills implied through action? Are some of the skills observable only beyond the classroom? Below we address some of these questions through examples and description.

## WHAT DATA LITERACY LOOKS LIKE

We have been observing teachers using data to help us understand how the knowledge, skills, and dispositions that comprise data literacy for teachers are manifested and how readily they can be recognized in practice. Some of the skills may be more apparent in the course of collaborative inquiry, that is, during data team activities. For example, in a data teaming environment, it may be easier to observe how teachers articulate or communicate about a problem of practice or how they understand contextual issues. Some of the skills may be explicit, and thus be observable from individual teachers in their classrooms; others may be inferred from teachers' behavior (e.g., how they monitor student performance, whether they use multiple sources of data, how they make instructional adjustments). Some of the skills may even be witnessed more readily outside of the classroom, such as after school when teachers may be examining and analyzing data using technological applications. We explore the differences.

**Data Teaming.** Collaborative inquiry during data team meetings is becoming more common. Teams can be formed in many different ways: by grade, by course, vertically within an elementary school, horizontally across content areas, or even across schools. Data teaming provides colleagues with an opportunity to examine data together and discuss the implications of the findings. As Means and colleagues (2011) note, it is also possible that teaming helps compensate for individual teachers' lack of data skills; that is, the process is so powerful that teachers can benefit from the collaboration.

Here is an example of data teaming:

Several teachers from a charter school come together to discuss how to address certain students' learning and behavioral issues. The teachers cross content domains. There are teachers from science, language arts, physical education, music, and career and technical education. The team notes that certain students are more prone to be absent or manifest behavioral problems. These same students seem to be struggling academically. They are chronically absent or are inattentive in class. The data team examines the patterns of absences, medical issues, and behavioral incidents, as well as performance in their classes. One finding is that many of these students rely on public transportation to get to school, with commutes of nearly an hour and with a few bus transfers. Another finding is that many of the students help their families financially by taking on one or two afterschool jobs, so they come to school exhausted. It is clear that their performance is suffering due to contextual factors that impede their ability to focus on what is happening in the classroom. The teachers recognize that some contextual issues are beyond their control, like the need for jobs to help support the students' families. The teachers discuss possible solutions to the contextual issues that in turn may stimulate better performance, including the use of mobile devices to facilitate anytime, anywhere learning opportunities or assistance in transportation that would minimize the challenges of getting to school.

This example shows that teachers need to contextualize their decision making around factors that may impact student performance. Many sources of data other than test scores or even in-class performance come into play here. The team has *identified a problem of practice* by contextualizing the issue at the student level but also at the school level. They must be aware of student privacy and confidentiality in their discussion of the issues, yet they may involve stakeholders (a parent, a guardian, a social worker, and so on) as needed. They have explicitly *framed a question* around the problem of practice. The exploration of data involves the *use data* and *transform data into information* components as depicted in Figures 3.5 and 3.6. The discussion centers on how to *transform the information into a decision* that will address the problem, trying to determine next steps for the teachers and plan for what happens in their classrooms. Once they have put the plans into action, they will *evaluate the outcomes* for intended and unintended consequences. If they have not succeeded, they will make another pass through the inquiry process to try and find another solution.

**In the Classroom.** The classroom is where a full range of decisions occurs, from moment-to-moment decisions based on a formative assessment process to more long-term decisions that are more summative in nature. Teachers are collecting and analyzing data on the spot, all the time in their classrooms, whether they realize it or not. It may be an observation of a student's level of engagement from body posture, to determination of student understanding through questioning, to diagnosis of a suspected physical problem, to a more formal examination of cognitive performance on an assessment or exercise. Teachers must be almost ringmasters in an always-evolving, multidimensional space that makes up the classroom. They may be providing individual attention to a struggling student. They may be working with one group of students while other students are doing something completely different. They may be doing an activity with the entire class.

Take, for example, the following scenario:

A high school mathematics teacher is working with his calculus class. He teaches in an economically challenged part of an urban area. Many students come from impoverished homes. Many students speak both English and Spanish. This is a top-notch class in the high school. The students are striving to gain scholarships to college and have excelled in their course work, despite external challenges. The teacher notices that recently one student who had a good record of performance was starting to struggle. The teacher had recently given a test on a particular topic in the curriculum. Most students had done quite well. A few students did not do so well, including this one student whose performance fell markedly. The teacher used the data from the assessment to reteach the concept, focusing on providing additional and targeted assistance to the students who had not met expectations. The reteaching helped all but the one student. The teacher delved further into what was happening with the student and found out that his father had recently left home. His mother needed financial assistance so the student had taken on two after-school jobs to help support the family. It was no wonder he was tired and his performance began to lag. The teacher therefore had a better understanding of why the student suddenly began to struggle and began to devise a plan of action to help the student.

In this example, the teacher had to identify the problem of practice and use many contextual factors to understand the situation. To remedy the problem, he had to involve various stakeholders, which might have included help from social services in consultation with the parent all the while, making sure to protect the student in terms of privacy. The teacher sought out diverse sources of data to find the cause of the problem. Within the classroom, he both differentiated and individualized instruction based on the diagnosis of student needs. The data were transformed into instructional actions around which he monitored the outcomes and results and determined if further intervention and action steps were required. He critically analyzed the situation using the iterative inquiry process.

**Outside the Classroom.** Teachers also use data outside of the classroom. They examine student work products during their free periods, after school, and at home. Time away from the classroom is likely to provide the opportunity for teachers to really dive into the data, either through a technology-based application or by hand. For example, teachers may do deep dives into the results of a classroom project by looking at the student responses during their planning period. Teachers may access their data system after school or from home to examine the patterns of results from a spot quiz to see how the students have done and identify possible topics for reteaching. Depending on the data systems teachers have in their classroom, some of this work could be done in real time, but more comprehensive dives into the data might need to be after class.

Take, for example, a teacher who has access to an assessment system that provides real-time data while students are taking an online assessment. During class, the teacher can monitor how students are doing as they are taking the test. She can see the responses, down to the level of the item response (i.e., whether the students selected the correct response or a distractor—an option on a multiple choice test that reflects an incorrect response—and even which distractor). She can see how the class did by item and how each student did across items, linked to a particular standard. A quick glance of the data display provides a broad-brush view of her class and individual students. It provides insights into how to structure instruction for the next day. But she wants to examine more deeply the item-level data to understand misconceptions and determine how best to remediate the learning issues. That requires more time than the quick analysis in the classroom. The teacher then accesses the results from home later in the day to gain a more in-depth picture of her students and the class. She also accesses additional sources of data, including past performance related to the test. She looks at attendance data. She takes into consideration the students' special status and other indicators that might be relevant.

Let us examine what skills are involved in this example. The teacher identifies the possible sources of data, what data are applicable or not, and understands the purposes of the different types of data sources. She accesses the data, uses multiple sources of data, both qualitative and quantitative, and probably checks for data quality and out-of-range data (e.g., a score of 110 is out of range when 100 is the maximum possible score). The teacher then integrates data sources and manipulates, examines, prioritizes, and organizes the data. She uses different sources of assessment data. She uses a technology system to access and analyze the data. She uses diagnostic skills and likely tests some assumptions or hypotheses. In the course of the analyses, the teacher is likely to use some statistics, examine some data displays or representations, and examine patterns and trends. She synthesizes the diverse data and summarizes them. She is likely to interpret the findings and draw inferences from them. These inquiry processes will lead to planning next steps in her instructional practice. It is possible that she will communicate with various audiences about her findings, including students, colleagues, and parents. All of these skills are incorporated into a single night's examination of some student performance results.

***"I'm Not Doing Data-Driven Decision Making, or Am I?"*** A teacher was asked if he was doing data-driven decision making in his classroom. He was a first-year science teacher with an undergraduate degree in the sciences and a Masters of Teaching. The teacher's response was a resounding "No." He reported that he did not have time in the evening to pull up students' scores and crank through the data to see how his students were performing. In his eyes, data-driven decision making required the actual access to data in a data system and the examination of them through a formal analytic process.

The teacher was asked a slightly different set of questions in the wake of his response. Okay, you don't have time to get onto the data system. But in your classroom, you ask students questions. You monitor their responses. You observe their reactions, attitudes, and level of engagement. You note if they are alert, engaged, sleepy, not feeling well, or not paying attention. From the responses, can't you determine if the students understand the problem or if they have some sort of misconception?

The answer was, "Of course." And can't you tell if they are attending to your instruction, may be distracted, or are not engaged? "Well, yes." The teacher was then asked to reconsider his initial response. Were these not sources of data—that is, the formative assessment process, the classroom observations, attention, motivation, engagement? The teacher pondered the question and without hesitating, said, "Yes, these are important sources of data." He further elaborated and noted that he assumed that data-driven decision making required quantitative data, real numbers that could be analyzed statistically.

A number of important points can be drawn from this example. First, one wonders if the science background of the teacher influenced the view of what data are and the inquiry process. To this teacher, data were purely quantitative. In this teacher's view, if he wasn't actually "analyzing the numbers," then he was not doing data-driven decision making. In actuality, teachers are using data all the time. They are accumulating data while observing a class, asking students questions, noting that a student is actively engaged in a learning activity, feeling ill, or misbehaving. Data come from many sources, expected and unexpected. Some data may provide direct indications of student performance while others may provide contextual information. Data-driven decision making need not occur on a technological tool. It can happen in a teacher's head, as was the case prior to the advent of many of the new and powerful technological applications. Good teachers have been using data forever. It is our conception of what data are and what is data-driven decision making that must be made clearer. Hopefully, we have made some progress in helping educators understand that the term *data* should be considered broadly to qualitative as well as quantitative sources and to diverse data, not just assessments and student performance.

## CHARTING A PATHWAY TOWARD ACTION

In Chapter 7 we discussed how various organizations and agencies interact to impact teacher professional development. We recap here steps that these agencies can take to facilitate the inclusion of the skills and knowledge of data literacy into the preparation of teachers. We reinforce the notion of how complex and systemic this change process is in the reality of practice. Change won't come easily or in the short term. We focus on proximal steps that can lead to the more distal objective of data-literate educators.

### Policymakers

As noted in earlier chapters, policymakers have been urging that education becomes an evidence-based profession for well over a decade. State licensure organizations are putting some requirements for teacher preparation programs, but for the most part there has been only rhetoric from policy-makers and professional organizations: "Teachers must use data." Federal education officials have spoken widely about the need for increased use of data but have done very little to provide resources to help build the human capacity for data use. The emphasis instead has been on building the state and federal technological data infrastructure. Only in the recent past (U.S. Department of Education, 2015) has the Request for Funding (RFP) for the Statewide Longitudinal Data Systems Grant Program focused on data use rather than technology per se. But still lacking in the RFP is a priority to help states develop data literacy among state and district staff. It must be clear by now that we feel strongly that educators at both the state and local levels need to know not just how to use the technological solutions to support data-driven decision making, but also how to use the data that reside in the technologies; and those data must be easily accessible, useful, and actionable. They also need to know how to use data that do not reside in data systems.

The most recent Comprehensive Center work includes seven content foci, and one of these is data-based decision making. This program is perhaps the only federally funded effort to build capacity around data use. One of the objectives of the Comprehensive Centers is to provide technical assistance to state departments of education, rather than direct assistance to districts. If a state wants to improve aspects of its data use, the Comprehensive Centers can provide technical assistance (U.S. Department of Education, 2012).

A small number of states have built into their recent SLDS grants the funds to provide for professional development workshops around data use as they continue to enhance their state data systems. But funds are sparse, and models to blanket an entire state are expensive and perhaps impossible. There have been some board-scale state efforts, some of which have gone forward and others have been dropped.

- Massachusetts and Maryland both released RFPs around training educators to use data and then withdrew them.
- Delaware has had a comprehensive program to train educators to use data for a number of years. As officials there note, they have had an abundance of riches. They also have had legislative support to spur the improvement of teacher preparation and the subsequent development of courses at the University of Delaware to increase educator data literacy.
- Arizona has developed a rubric of skills based on the Data Quality Campaign's (2014b) definition of what it means to be a data-literate educator and informed by our work. Its licensure staff has begun working with the colleges of education throughout the state to have them endorse the rubric. The staff is working most closely with the University of Arizona to integrate data literacy into the teacher

preparation program there. Independently, a professor at Arizona State University is developing a five-course sequence for graduate-level classes.

- The Virginia Department of Education was perhaps one of the first and most forward thinking state education agency to consider data use and require educators to know how to use data. As early as 2008, the superintendent of instruction incorporated data literacy into the state licensure and certification requirements (Virginia Board of Education, 2008). The Commonwealth of Virginia (2015) appears to be very serious about broad-scale professional development around data use. It released a Request for Information to professional development providers to explore the possibility of providing "professional development for the use of data to improve instruction" for their "132 school districts, 2,092 public schools, 3,376 counselors, 96,647 teachers and 3,991 school administrators and there are an estimated 50 DOE staff" (p. 4).

All this progress by states is significant, but not sufficient. States that have adopted the InTASC standards (2013a) are steeped in data skills (Mandinach, Friedman, & Gummer, 2015). However, the inclusion of data skills into state standards may not be a strong enough incentive for schools of education to include data literacy in their curricula. It is clear that some states have done a better job than others in both talking abut the importance of data use as well as taking steps to affect change.

So what further action should policymakers take? At the federal level, we urge policymakers to continue to speak about the importance of data use and evidence-based practice. If they continue to make it clear how important data use is, other stakeholder groups will understand that this is not a passing fad, but it is a necessary part of educational practice. But these policymakers must go further than just talking the talk. They must mandate that educators become data literate, and if necessary, put into place accountability measures that require changes in practice. Foremost, they must provide funding and resources to make possible the preparation and training of educators. This could be done through subsequent RFPs for the SLDSs, the Comprehensive Centers, the Regional Education Laboratories, and other federal programs that impact state and local levels.

At the state level, policymakers could follow the model Virginia has put into place: Mandate the demonstration of data literacy for certification and licensure. Consider broad professional development across the state for all educators at the state departments of education and in the districts. Insist that the agency responsible for licensure and certification (sometimes within the state department or in a parallel agency, such as in Kentucky and Oregon) revise their documentation to include explicit statements about data literacy skills and knowledge, not just assessment literacy.

One concrete step that states can take to help teacher preparation programs is to provide simulated data sets like those generated by their data systems to familiarize educators with the kinds of data they will encounter in practice. Arizona is doing this. Other states could emulate this practice by providing accessible resources to the teacher preparation programs.

## Professional Organizations

*American Association of Colleges for Teacher Education.* AACTE is a membership organization that represents roughly 800 colleges of education. According to the organization's website (AACTE, 2015), their mission is to advocate for and build "capacity for high-quality educator preparation programs in a dynamic landscape." AACTE's CEO and a staff member have participated in DQC events and working groups around data literacy. Recognizing the difficulty of engaging their membership, the organization could be more explicit in their advocacy on behalf of the data skill set. To date, however, AACTE has focused more on assessment literacy than data literacy. For example, they conducted three webinars in 2014 about assessment literacy (listed in Chapter 2). We urge the organization to think more broadly about the data that teachers need (not just assessment data) and begin to explore with its member institutions the steps needed to integrate data literacy into teacher preparation.

*Council for the Accreditation of Educator Preparation.* CAEP is responsible for the accreditation of teacher preparation programs. CAEP (2015) has developed standards against which schools of education are evaluated and certified. It is clear that CAEP understands the need for introducing data literacy into teacher preparation. Jim Cibulka (2013), a former CAEP president, has spoken broadly about education as a data-driven practice. A Blue Ribbon Panel convened by NCATE (2010), now known as part of CAEP, produced 10 recommendations about the clinical practice of educators, including three that pertain to data use. In 2014, CAEP included an invited panel on data literacy for its annual convention that was widely attended (Mandinach, Kowalski, Ashdown, & Orland, 2014). In 2015, the senior leadership expanded that invitation to include a preconference workshop for deans, associate deans, and assessment leaders (Mandinach & Gummer, 2015). The workshop repeated in 2016. There were two objectives for the workshops. First, CAEP sought to get data literacy front and center for this audience, addressing what the construct is and what it will take to get it into teacher preparation programs. Second, the organization sought to help the audience understand the need for them to use data for organizational continuous improvement. CAEP's standards are replete with the use of data for metrics around programmatic improvement. They model the kind of data-driven decision making in which schools of education must engage and the data literacy that their graduates must exhibit in their practice.

***National Board for Professional Teaching Standards.*** The NBPTS is the organization that sets the standards for teacher board certification, laying out the skills and knowledge "accomplished teachers" need to be able to demonstrate. The board certification process is rigorous and voluntary, with very few teachers (2%) attaining their certification (Thorpe, 2014). National Board Standards (2015) are based on five key propositions, in 25 certificate areas.

The National Board also had a staff member on the DQC data literacy working group. It arranged a special symposium for the working group at its 2014 conference (Mandinach, Kowalski, Farley-Ripple, Atkins, & George, 2014). It included the DQC's vice president for policy, a researcher, a professor who has been developing a course on data literacy for teachers, a data-oriented teacher, and a superintendent who created a strong data culture within her district. The audience did not want to hear about policy, theory, or even teacher preparation. They wanted to hear from the boots-on-the-ground teacher and superintendent, asking them questions about what it will take to make data use a reality and what are the challenges. Having sessions like this, attended by around 400 educators, helps get the word out. It shows a level of endorsement by the National Board.

The National Board also included data literacy in its discussion of new standards. Mandinach was invited to serve on an expert panel that combined both data literacy and assessment literacy. The invitation was promising; it was a sign of recognition that data literacy should be a component of the skill sets needed by Board Certified Teachers. Although assessment literacy and assessment data predominate, including data literacy in the test specifications provides an important opportunity to make an explicit message to the field that teachers need to know how to use *all* data, not just assessment data.

So what can the National Board do? It can continue to include sessions about data literacy at its conference. It can invite a keynote speech on data literacy rather than a concurrent session. Its leadership can include data literacy as part of speaking points and in objective statements with the goal to improve the professionalism of teaching as a profession. The NBPTS can become an advocate for the data-literate teacher. The NBPTS can ensure that data literacy has a place in the standards for board certification, recognizing that teachers need to understand how to use all sorts of data.

***National Association of State Directors of Teacher Education and Certification.*** NASDTEC represents the individuals and boards within state education agencies that deal with standards for licensure and certification. In that capacity, state representatives to NASDTEC are in the position to urge states to incorporate specific language into their licensure and certification documentation. Their executive director, Phil Rogers, was part of the DQC working group on data literacy and has recognized the construct's importance. Data literacy was included as part of the 2013 annual conference as a main session (Kowalski, 2013; Mandinach, 2013) to help educate the members about the importance of the then emerging construct. As noted above, states vary in how they address data literacy skills and knowledge (Mandinach, Friedman, & Gummer 2015). Some states are very explicit, whereas others lack specificity. Some states do not even address data literacy. Some states conflate data literacy with assessment literacy. It is safe to say that it is important for states to incorporate the skills and knowledge of data literacy into their regulations as they are revised. These regulations, in turn, will communicate the importance to schools of education that their candidates and graduates must acquire this skill set.

Thus it is essential for NASDTEC members to incorporate the language of data literacy for teachers into their state certification regulations. Teacher preparation programs pay attention to these regulations. To date, the language is cursory in many states and lacks specificity. Including a specific data standard may be too much to ask. Including specific skills around data use could be easily accomplished. Additionally, the regulations should distinguish between data literacy and assessment literacy. NASDTEC could again include a keynote speech or workshop at its annual conference to help members gain a better understanding of data literacy and how to integrate the skill set into the regulations.

*Other Professional Organizations.* Other professional associations such as those for school boards (National Association of State Boards of Education), teachers (National Education Association and American Federation of Teachers), and school and district leaders (National Association of Elementary School Principals, National Association of Secondary School Principals, National Association of Middle School Principals, and American Association of School Administrators) all have a role in enculturating data literacy in districts. The professional organizations need to take a position on the issue of data literacy and advocate for training and preparation around data use—namely, that teachers, administrators, and even school boards must know how to use data and be consumers of information. They must not only take a stand, they must publicize and model it by inviting experts to their annual conventions as speakers in prominent roles. Policymakers, researchers, or others need to work with organizational leadership to obtain keynotes, conduct workshops, or find other ways to gain the attention of the associations' membership.

## Schools of Education

For several years now, whenever Mandinach begins a workshop or a speech with educators, she opens with a question to the audience, "How many of you have taken a course on data-driven decision making in your education career?" Most times, the audience is silent. Sometimes a few hands will be raised, but when probed about the courses, they turn out to be assessment courses. Infrequently, someone will say they have taken a data course and it turns out to indeed be a data course. It is rare. It needs to become the norm rather than the exception.

Schools of education can contribute to the change process in two ways. First and foremost, they can introduce data literacy into their curricula for teachers and leaders in an integrated manner or as stand-alone courses. Second, graduate schools of education can produce future professors who can teach the stand-alone courses and can work with other faculty to integrate data use into both content and methods courses and practical experiences.

We suspect that change will not come easily to schools of education. There are many legitimate challenges. In conversations with administrators at schools of education, we have heard many legitimate reasons for why introducing data literacy into programs is so challenging, including the following:

- We don't have anyone who can teach a data course.
- If we are going to hire a faculty member, data-driven decision making is not sufficiently important when there are many other more pressing faculty slots to fill.
- Our faculty are unwilling to change and integrate data use into existing courses.
- Our faculty do not know enough about data use to carry out such integration.
- We have no wiggle room in our curriculum for a course on data.
- There are no good materials that can be used in courses, either stand-alone or with an integrated model.
- Existing materials are more amenable to professional development than university courses.
- We do not have data sets that can be used to familiarize the teacher candidates with state data.
- We might be able to do a leadership course on data, but preparing teachers is just too difficult.

And these are just a few of the challenges. But with time, the field can begin to address them. The old light bulb joke applies here: How many psychologists does it take to change a light bulb? One, but the light bulb must want to change. Schools of education must change. If they don't, the concern is that the accountability hammer will come slamming down on them. So what must schools of education do? They must be willing to make changes to address this need and recognize that data use is no longer a passing fad. They must work with state and local education agencies to understand the need. From the state agencies, they can understand what skills and knowledge are required in regulations. From the districts, they can understand what is actually needed in the real world of practice. Some districts are now requiring educators to demonstrate their ability to use data as part of the hiring process. This should impact what the schools of education do. They can use models from some institutions that have been able to integrate data into their curriculum (Mandinach & Friedman, 2015). They can seek out experts in the field of research to become informed about what data literacy is. As noted in Chapter 7, they can seek out some of the good models of professional development that have transitioned their professional development into university courses (e.g., the Data Wise Project at Harvard creating a MOOC and a course in the school of education) or have developed online versions that could be widely disseminated, particularly for graduate-level courses (e.g., the virtual version of TERC's Using Data Project). They can seek to hire professors and adjuncts who can teach stand-alone courses or work with existing faculty to assist in the integration of data literacy into methods and content courses. They can even reach out to local school districts for someone who could teach about data based on their practical experiences (e.g., the University of Virginia's collaboration with Charlottesville Public Schools).

As Peck and McDonald (2014) note, creating evidence-based practices in schools of education is not an easy task. It is fraught with impediments and challenges. But not unlike enculturating data-driven decision making into schools and districts, many of the same concepts and resources can be generalized to schools of education. In fact, the parallels are quite striking. There is a need for strong leadership with an explicit vision for data use. There is a need to understand the purpose of data use, the intended objectives, and the idea that data must be both useful and actionable. There is a need for a collaborative inquiry process, much like data teams in schools, with distributed leadership. Such teaming requires common meeting time that is focused and structured. There is a need for a data system to support the programmatic improvement process. There must be an open and trusting environment that includes room for dissent, conflict, and frank discussions based on data. There must be a common language that undergirds the inquiry process. Finally, the use of data must become a routinized or integrated part of practice.

## Local Education Agencies

School boards must recognize that all educational staff should have at least some level of knowledge about how to use data. This includes administrators, teachers, and even data clerks. They can provide support for professional development, training, and other resources to facilitate the use of data in their districts. They can model the use of data by making decisions based on evidence rather than political expedience. Superintendents must make clear that there is an expectation that educators within their districts must know how to use data effectively and responsibly. This expectation, in conjunction with an explicit vision for data use, can impact not only practice but also hiring decisions. Such decisions can impact the schools of education from which new teachers or administrators are hired. For example, some school districts require candidates for principal positions to be able to demonstrate data literacy through the administration of authentic assessments that require them to develop school improvement plans from simulated data sets (Long et al., 2008). If school districts make clear that they will be reluctant to hire candidates from particular schools of education where data literacy is not a part of preparation, then those institutions may be stimulated into action to respond to the needs of the districts. Building and district leaders must model data use and make explicit the requirements that their current and future staff must be data literate.

### Parents and Students

Parents and students also can play a role. They must demand that the educators that serve their community be evidence-based. They must expect teachers to use evidence provided by data to inform instructional practice. They must expect teachers and administrators to discuss student performance based on data, not just anecdotes or gut feelings. A reciprocal relationship may well exist. Teachers can help students become their own data-driven decision makers, as recommended in the IES Practice Guide (Hamilton et al., 2009), but they in turn can expect their teachers to also use data. Ideally, parents and students must understand the power data have to inform educational practice.

### Testing Organizations

As noted in Chapter 7, testing organizations play a role in affecting change through an accountability process that requires teacher candidates to demonstrate that they know how to use data. Assessments must be informed by research during the development process. Until recently, there was no common language on which to build test specifications. Now that the field has working definitions of data literacy (Data Quality Campaign, 2014b; Gummer & Mandinach, 2015) and specifications of the skills and knowledge that comprise the construct (Gummer & Mandinach, 2015; Mandinach, Friedman, & Gummer, 2015), the tests must incorporate this work to reflect the current knowledge in the field of data-driven decision making. Schools of education will heed the inclusion of the data literacy knowledge and skills on tests. The Stanford Center for Assessment, Learning and Equity, the developers of the edTPA, should consider introducing data literacy, not just assessment literacy. Assessment literacy is one of the scales in the edTPA, but the *Assessment Task* and its rubrics could be expanded to consider other forms of data beyond assessment data, thereby also measuring data literacy.

## Researchers

Researchers can provide valuable information to practitioners and policy-makers about various aspects of data-driven decision making, including implementation and impact. Implementation studies can describe the processes needed for successfully enculturating data use into practice. Impact studies can provide evidence of the outcomes that result from data use. The findings from research studies on data-driven decision making and data literacy also can be translated into the development of materials and resources that can aid in the preparation of educators to use data.

*Research to Inform Decisions About Practice.* Research has an important role in rolling out data literacy in practice. It forms the basis for understanding what data literacy is and what the skills and knowledge that comprise the construct are. As we have noted, the construct is still evolving as the field continues to gain a more in-depth understanding of what it means to use data effectively and responsibly. Yet there are still a number of components of data literacy still to be methodically explored. Also as noted earlier, we don't know the optimal time or place to introduce data to educators. Data use can be a complete abstraction if introduced too early. For example, a teacher may be provided a set of results with no background about the content or context of the information, but there needs to be contextual information to ground the teacher's understanding of the meaning of the results. Introducing data too late may be an impediment to its becoming a deeply embedded or enculturated part of teachers' repertoires. We don't know what the minimum level of data literacy should be. For example, we would have to examine all of the knowledge and skills outlined in Chapters 3 and 4 to determine what is the most basic level that could be considered acceptable as data literate. We have a sense of what a data expert looks like. Similarly, we would need to look at the upper level of the developmental continua for the skills to determine what sophisticated use looks like. We also have a sense of what incompetence is. We suspect, however, that not everyone needs to be a data nerd. In fact, some educators, such as superintendents, may need to be more consumers of information than data users. A consumer of information is someone who does not actually work with the raw data, but instead is given synthesized information in the form of reports. The skill set is likely to be a bit different in terms of understanding information that someone else has analyzed. But how much is enough and how little is too little? Thus we need to define minimum competency. We need to outline expertise. Then we need to trace the development from data novice to data native.

We need to understand the role-based nature of data literacy: Are there skills specific to teachers, principals, superintendents, and other administrators? How does the construct for teachers in Figure 3.3 generalize to other educators? Many of the different domains pertain only to teachers, but are there similar domains that lay out the knowledge for administrators? The difference between the identified skills in our framework for data literacy for teachers that focuses solely on teachers and the much more general outline provided by the SLDS State Support Group (2015) is obvious. This group is comprised of data directors from state departments of education and school districts. Their intent was to outline a more generic set of skills for data use in education, regardless of what role individuals play in the education system. Within the domain of teaching, we need to explore the role of content and pedagogical expertise. As we have discussed, there is an obvious interplay among data use and content and pedagogical content knowledge. We need to know what impact teachers' levels of content knowledge has on how they use data. Similarly, we need to understand the impact of data skills on how teachers apply their pedagogical content knowledge and visa versa. Individuals may be expert data analysts, but they may have insufficient knowledge of their domain or of the instructional strategies that can be applied, thereby affecting the impact of the data use. Is there a level of domain knowledge below which data use will not make sense? What happens if teachers have data skills and understand their content, but lack the pedagogical content knowledge to take instructional action?

Finally, how can research inform the integration of data literacy for teachers into content and methods courses in schools of education? One way is to understand the extent to which the knowledge and skills that comprise the "data literacy for teachers" construct (see Chapter 3) are actually addressed in current courses or where they best can be integrated. This would almost become a diagnostic process with professors. Professors would be forced to consider if and how each of the skills or knowledge are addressed in their courses, and where they might be integrated. Researchers can help develop data sets, exercises, scenarios, and instruments that can be used by professors, professional development providers, district workshop providers, and others for training and assessment purposes. For example, professional development providers have designed for training purposes scenarios or situations that teachers are likely to encounter in their classes (see Love et al., 2008). These scenarios contain contextual information to ground the teachers' understanding of the situation. They contain simulated raw data like the data that teachers would see in their classrooms. Together, these form the basis for exercises that help teachers step through the data inquiry cycle depicted in Figure 3.4.

*Development of Curricular Materials.* The accumulation of information and evidence about good practices related to data use is a necessary foundation for the development of curricular materials that can be used in schools of education. These would be materials based on the knowledge, skills, and dispositions outlined in Chapters 3 and 4 that can be integrated into content and methods courses or combined into stand-alone courses on data use. So far there have been few existing data courses that were truly data courses, not assessment courses (Mandinach, Friedman, & Gummer, 2015). Some of the courses, particularly those at the graduate level, use existing books that were intended for professional development audiences rather than preservice students. The structure differs. Professional development tends to focus on how to execute general skills. It does not typically delve into theory, purposes, or rationales. Professional development providers may not have knowledge of all content areas, and rarely address how to transform data into information and then into actionable instructional steps. Based on our analyses, few resources and materials have been available that fit nicely in preservice preparation programs, and even fewer show evidence of an understanding of the skills and knowledge that comprise data literacy for teachers (Mandinach & Gummer, 2012, 2013b); that is, the materials fail to explicitly describe these essential components of data literacy. Existing books are how-to manuals that may not be applicable as course content and fare better in professional development.

Thus there is a pressing need for the development of materials that can be used as a course or in a course, that is, to support a stand-alone course or be integrated into existing courses, including content (e.g., science, math, social studies) and methods classes (e.g., instructional methods). The materials should be developed based on knowledge culled from current research on data use in education and best practices from the field. They should be based on models that seem to work from emerging programs (Mandinach & Friedman, 2015). Chapter 5 outlined the key components for integrating data literacy into teacher preparation programs. These include vision, sustained leadership, a feedback loop with participating school districts, and integration into content and methods courses, as well as clinical experiences. Ideally, the materials should be maximally flexible, grounded in emerging technologies such as mobile devices, and deliverable virtually as well as in person in formal courses. They should be developed with various audiences in mind, including teacher preparation programs, graduate programs, professional development providers, school districts, and educators.

We basically have a chicken and egg issue here. Courses can't be taught without materials. Professors and practitioners may not perceive a need for data courses or data integrated into courses unless materials and data sets are available. Yet the substantial investment in the development of materials may not be feasible unless there is a niche and a need. Build it and they will come? Perhaps. They won't come if we don't build it, that's for sure. The field of education needs to break up this challenge and move forward to provide quality materials to stakeholder groups.

## Other Stakeholder Groups

*Data Quality Campaign.* The DQC, as a nonpartisan advocacy organization that supports the use of data in education, has transitioned their focus from examining the evolution of the state data systems to addressing the use of data at the local, state, and federal levels. This transition reflects the changing priorities from building the technological infrastructure to data use and the human capacity to use the data. The DQC has convened several working groups, including one that focused on what it means to be a data-literate teacher. Two concurrent events sponsored by the DQC launched data literacy into the public's attention. The DQC forum (2014a) gave national attention to data literacy, while the data literacy white paper (2104b) provided a general definition to inform policymakers and other stakeholders. The DQC continues to advocate about the importance of data literacy to all who will listen and even those who may not believe in data use. They are positioned to leverage change and must continue to do so. We commend their efforts and will continue to work with them toward the ultimate goal of data literacy in education.

*Professional Development Providers.* Professional development providers are helping prepare current educators to use data. Their work and knowledge can be translated in part to the realm of teacher preparation. Materials for teacher preparation may need to be more explicit in terms of explanations and context, things that more experienced teachers may take for granted. The materials made need to be simplified in terms of content or instructional methods with which teacher candidates may not be familiar. Most certainly, the educators who are likely to be in professional development workshops have had some or substantial classroom experience that will help them concretize the context of the training. Preservice preparation is different. Teacher candidates have not had the opportunity or experience of being in a classroom so their lenses to the use of data will differ.

Providers should consider how they might be able to modify their materials and models in ways there are amendable to preservice preparation. For example, materials that are geared to experienced teachers may be too sophisticated in terms of real-world situations that they may have encountered, in contrast to teacher candidates, who have no such experience. Providers need to determine the level of engagement on the part of students and how that engagement potentially impacts learning and behavior. They can work with schools of education to develop materials that could be integrated into graduate-level courses. They might even be able to provide virtual courses for students through affiliations with schools of education, when it is impossible for the institutions to provide a course on their own or they cannot integrate data use into existing course structures.

## CONCLUSION

We have covered a great deal of territory in this book. It is almost 53 shades of data for the number of skills and knowledge we have identified. We have laid out a conceptual framework for data literacy for teachers in Chapters 3 and 4, complete with the skills, knowledge, and dispositions that comprise data literacy for teachers and make an educator data literate. We have grounded the use of data in current policy, noting that data-driven decision making is not a panacea, and in fact, has vocal opponents. We have noted that data use can no longer be considered a passing fad; it has become an essential component of educator practice. The use of data and evidence in education can lead to increased professionalism for teachers and administrators, like other disciplines such as medicine. Data-driven decision making is not new, but it is now an expected practice. Yet the field has suffered from inattention to the adequate preparation of preservice educators in particular, as well as sporadic training of current educators. This volume has attempted to operationalize the construct "data literacy for teachers" and what it will take to embed it in the preparation of teachers across the developmental continuum.

### How Data Literacy Will Change the Practice of Educators

We have always maintained that good teachers have been using data for a long time. One issue now is the expectation that educators use data to inform their practice. There also is the proliferation of data and the fact that there are technologies to facilitate data use that were not readily available even a decade ago. So, will data literacy change the practice of educators? The answer may be both yes and no.

Teachers still use their knowledge to inform what and how they teach. With domains becoming more systematically laid out through learning progressions that map the intended trajectories of learning in a content area, data use can help teachers navigate the learning trajectories. Data can tell teachers where students are in terms of targeted cognitive and noncognitive topics, and what they know and don't know. Technologies can link student performance in real time to standards and help teachers identify immediately where learning deficits exist and what content needs to be taught or retaught. Technologies such as data dashboards can provide essential information that allows teachers to carefully monitor individual students and groups of students. These technologies can drill down to levels of analysis immediately that would take teachers hours to do. Further, the diverse sources of data that can allow teachers to triangulate among the sources and contextual issues might not be possible without the technological support.

Administrators also must be data literate to inform their decision making. The "data literacy for teachers" construct, as we have explained in Chapter 3 and in Figures 3.3 through 3.7, is targeted at the transformations teachers must make from their data, embedding the results in a content domain and ultimately into instructional action. The knowledge and skills that pertain specifically to the instructional process may not be necessary for administrators, but they must be aware of these skills. In particular, skills like making instructional adjustments and determining instructional next steps are obviously more applicable to teaching. That said, many of the knowledge and skills found among the other components—identifying a problem of practice and framing a question, using data, transforming data into information, and evaluating outcomes—all are relevant to decision making by administrators. In terms of the domains of knowledge, administrators also need to know about educational contexts, learner characteristics, content, pedagogy, and educational purposes. That knowledge may not be manifested in classroom practice as it would be for teachers, but it is relevant for administrators as well. Additionally, there will be domains of knowledge specifically for administrators that will interact with the data-use skills. It may be knowledge of how to handle personnel, financial, curricular, transportation, and other topics that are relevant to specific administrative decision making.

One subtle change might be found in the role of the student. An objective is for students to be their own data-driven decision makers (Hamilton et al., 2009). Bringing students into the mix requires them to take responsibility for their own learning in ways that heretofore were not expected. The expectation is that they become more engaged. The technologies found in blended learning environments enable students to learn anytime and anywhere (Baker, 2014; Bienkowski, 2014; DiCerbo & Behrens, 2014; Dieterle, 2014). And teachers can monitor their performance in real time. The technological tools make possible the granularity of the data that are produced from the microanalytics that reside in the technologies.

## The Effect of the Enculturation of Data Use

Teacher candidates learn many things in their preparation programs. They try out theory and methods in their practical experiences. Inservice teachers gain additional skills and knowledge from professional development. Research has shown that professional development in data use must be ongoing rather than a one-time event (Means et al., 2010). Earl and Katz

(2006) have made clear that if educators think that using data is an isolated activity, then they are not doing data-driven decision making properly. The effective use of data must be an enculturated method, a tool that is deeply embedded in all practice, and an ongoing process. The concern, however, is the sustainability of the skills provided in coursework or through professional development. School cultures are very strong. As we know from the IES Practice Guide (Hamilton et al., 2009), a critical review of the literature on data-driven decision making, there are a number of very important resources and supports that are needed in schools and districts for data use to take hold and become a sustained process. They include the provision for data teams, data coaches, common planning time, technologies that facilitate data use, an explicit vision for data use, and leadership, among others. As described in Chapter 1, a data team is a group of educators who meet as a team to examine data and discuss the implications for their practice. Data coaches are typically individuals who understand how to use data and can effectively take a leadership role and facilitate data use among colleagues. If teacher candidates receive data literacy preparation in their coursework and field experiences, then it may be difficult for the new teachers to function effectively in terms of data-driven decision making in a school where there is no data culture with its supports. If there is a history of data, the new teachers can slip into the functioning data culture quite easily. Schools must sustain what educators have learned in their preparation. We can't expect new teachers to be lone wolves. These individuals certainly can use data as has been learned, but there still need to be organizational resources to support that practice.

There are actually three interdependent levels of enculturation. The skills must be embedded within teachers' repertoires and supported by their schools and districts. The districts must enculturate and embrace data-driven decision making. And finally, schools of education, like the districts, must enculturate the notion of data use. It is both data use for continuous programmatic improvement and data use as a part of educator preparation. We have made clear that schools of education do not function in isolation, but within a complex system surrounded by associated organizations and agencies.

## A Concluding Metaphor

We want to end by revisiting the metaphor mentioned in the previous chapter. Recall that Guidera (2013, 2014) has talked about systemic change in education around data use, differentiating between a hammer and a flashlight. The hammer represents the pressure of accountability. The flashlight, in contrast, illuminates the path toward enlightenment through the use of data. We apply the metaphor in two ways: to teachers and to schools of education. Increasingly, teachers must use data. They will need to demonstrate that ability on accountability measures such as Praxis, edTPA, or newly planned teacher licensure examinations. These are the hammers. The other option is for teachers to realize on their own that data use should and must become an embedded part of their practice. This is their flashlight. For schools of education, their hammer will be the poor performance of their graduates, thereby negatively affecting the institutional evaluation. The flashlight would be that schools of education determine, on their own, that data literacy is something that must be included in their teacher preparation programs. The change will come slowly and it won't be easy, but we are convinced it will be worthwhile. We strongly urge both teachers and schools of education to adopt the flashlight and avoid the hammer (see Figure 8.1). A lighted pathway to knowledge will serve them well in future practice, so bring on the flashlight!

**Figure 8.1. No More Hammers!**

# References

Aguerrebere, J. (2009, August). [Remarks]. Panel discussion on Alliance for Excellent Education's publication *A Wealth of Riches: Delivering on the Promise of Data to Transform Teaching and Learning* conducted at the Teachers' Use of Data to Impact Teaching and Learning Conference, Washington, DC.

American Association of Colleges for Teacher Education (AACTE). (2015). *About AACTE.* Retrieved from aacte.org/about-aacte

American Federation of Teachers (AFT). (2012). *Raising the bar: Aligning and elevating teacher preparation and the teaching profession.* Washington, DC: Author. Retrieved from http://www.aft.org/sites/default/files/news/raisingthebar2013.pdf

American Recovery and Reinvestment Act of 2009 (ARRA). Pub. L. No. 111-5, 123 Stat. 115 (2009). Retrieved from www.gpo.gov/fdsys/pkg/PLAW-111pub5content-detail.html

Arizona Department of Education. (2015). *AZDash: Accelerating student achievement.* Retrieved from www.azed.gov/aelas/az-dash/

Armstrong, J., & Anthes, K. (2001). How data can help: Putting information to work to raise student achievement. *American School Board Journal, 188*(1), 38–41.

Baker, R. (2014, April). *Toward demonstrating the value of learning analytics in education.* Paper presented at a presidential symposium at the annual meeting of the American Educational Research Association, Philadelphia, PA.

Bandura, A. (1977). *Social learning theory.* Englewood Cliffs, NJ: Prentice-Hall.

Bergan, J. R., Burnham, C. G., Bergan, J. R., Callahan, S. M., & Feld, J. K. (2013). *Composition of a comprehensive assessment system.* Tucson, AZ: Assessment Technology Incorporated.

Bettesworth, L. R., Alonzo, J., & Duesbery, L. (2008). Swimming in the depths: Educators' ongoing effective use of data to guide decision making. In T. J. Kowalski & T. J. Lasley II (Eds.), *Handbook of data-based decision making in education* (pp. 286–303). New York, NY: Routledge.

Bienkowski, M. (2014, April). *Putting the learner at the center: Exposing analytics to learning.* Paper presented at a presidential symposium at the annual meeting of the American Educational Research Association, Philadelphia, PA.

Boudett, K. P., City, E. A., & Murnane, R. J. (Eds.). (2013). *Data Wise: A step-by-step guide to using assessment results to improve teaching and learning* (Rev. ed.). Cambridge, MA: Harvard Education Press.

Boudett, K. P., & Steele, J. L. (Eds.). (2007). *Data Wise in action: Stories of schools using data to improve teaching and learning.* Cambridge, MA: Harvard Education Press.

Breaux, G. A., & Chepko, S. (2015, April). *Data and assessment literacy in schools of education.* Paper presented at the annual meeting of the American Educational Research Association, Chicago, IL.

Bridgman, P. W. (1959). *The way things are.* Cambridge, MA: Harvard University Press.

Brunner, C., Fasca, C., Heinze, J., Honey, M., Light, D., Mandinach, E. B., & Wexler, D. (2005). Linking data and learning: The Grow Network study. *Journal of Education for Students Placed at Risk, 10*(3), 241–267.

Canada, B., Dawson, E., & Bell, B. (2015, July). *Designing dynamic data use for districts by districts.* Paper presented at the 2015 NCES STATS-DC Data Conference, Washington, DC.

Carlson, D., Borman, G. D., Robinson, M. (2011). A multistate district-level cluster randomized trial of the impact of data-driven reform on reading and mathematics achievement. *Educational Evaluation and Policy Analysis, 33*(3), 378–398.

Center for Data-Driven Reform in Education (CDDRE). (2011). *CDDRE teaches a data-driven decision-making process.* Retrieved from www.cddre.org/

Chappuis, S., Stiggins, R. J., Arter, J. A., & Chappuis, J. (2009). *Assessment for learning: An action guide for school leaders* (2nd ed.). Boston, MA: Allyn & Bacon.

Chen, E., Heritage, M., & Lee, J. (2005). Identifying and monitoring students' learning needs with technology. *Journal of Education for Students Placed at Risk, 10*(3), 309–332.

Cibulka, J. (2013, August). Leveraging the InTASC standards and progressions. In *Next Generation Standards and Accreditation Policies for Teacher Preparation and Development* [Webinar]. Washington, DC: Alliance for Excellent Education.

Common Core State Standards Initiative. (2010). *Common Core State Standards for English language arts & literacy in history/social studies, science, and technical subjects.* Retrieved from www.corestandards.org/assets/CCSSI_ELA%20 Standards.pdf

Common Core State Standards Initiative. (2015a). *Common Core Standards.* Retrieved from www.corestandards.org/

Common Core State Standards Initiative. (2015b). *Common Core State Standards for mathematics.* Retrieved from http://www.corestandards.org/assets/CCSSI_ Math%20Standards.pdf

Commonwealth of Virginia. (2015). *Professional development for the use of data to improve instruction* (RFI NO. DOE-PD-2015-01). Richmond, VA: Author.

Confrey, J., & Makar, K. (2005). Critiquing and improving data use from high stakes tests: Understanding variation and distribution in relation to equity using dynamic statistics software. In C. Dede, J. P. Honan, & L. C. Peters (Eds.), *Scaling up success: Lessons learned from technology-based educational improvement* (pp. 198–226). San Francisco, CA: Jossey-Bass.

Copland, M. A., Knapp, M. S., & Swinnerton, J. A. (2009). Principal leadership, data, and school improvement. In T. J. Kowalski & T. J. Lasley II (Eds.), *Handbook of data-based decision making in education* (pp. 153–172). New York, NY: Routledge.

Council for the Accreditation of Educator Preparation (CAEP). (2013a). *CAEP accreditation standards.* Washington, DC: Author.

Council for the Accreditation of Educator Preparation (CAEP). (2013b). *CAEP accreditation standards of educator preparation.* Washington, DC: Author.

Council for the Accreditation of Educator Preparation (CAEP). (2015). *CAEP accreditation standards.* Washington, DC: Author.

Council of Chief State School Officers (CCSSO). (2012). *Our responsibility, our promise: Transforming educator preparation and entry into the profession.* Washington, DC: Author. Retrieved from http://www.ccsso.org/Documents/2012/Our%20Responsibility%20Our%20Promise_2012.pdf

Data Quality Campaign (DQC). (2011*). State analysis by state action: Action 9.* Retrieved from dataqualitycampaign.org/your-states-progress/10-state-actions?action=nine

Data Quality Campaign (DQC). (2012). *State analysis by state action: Action 9.* Retrieved from dataqualitycampaign.org/your-states-progress/10-state-actions?action=nine

Data Quality Campaign (DQC). (2013). *State analysis by state action: Action 9.* Retrieved from dataqualitycampaign.org/your-states-progress/10-state-actions?action=nine

Data Quality Campaign (DQC). (2014a, February). *Empowering teachers with data: Policies and practices to promote educator data literacy* [Forum and webcast]. Washington, DC: Data Quality Campaign. Retrieved from http://dataquality-campaign.org/blog/2014/01/new-video-event-empowering-teachers-through-data-literacy/

Data Quality Campaign (DQC). (2014b). *State analysis by state action: Action 9.* Retrieved from dataqualitycampaign.org/your-states-progress/10-state-actions?action=nine

Data Quality Campaign (DQC). (2014c). *Teacher data literacy: It's about time.* Washington, DC: Author. Retrieved from http://www.dataqualitycampaign.org/wp-content/uploads/files/DQC-Data%20Literacy%20Brief.pdf

Data Quality Campaign (DQC). (2014d, July). *What's the difference between assessment literacy and data literacy?* [Webinar]. Washington, DC: Author

Data Quality Campaign (DQC). (2015a). *Search results for "privacy."* Retrieved from dataqualitycampaign.org/?s=privacy

Data Quality Campaign (DQC). (2015b). *State analysis by essential elements.* Retrieved from dataqualitycampaign.org/your-states-progress/10-essential-elements/

Data Quality Campaign (DQC). (2015c). *State analysis by state action.* Retrieved from dataqualitycampaign.org/your-states-progress/10-state-actions/

Datnow, A., & Park, V. (2009). School system strategies for supporting data use. In T. J. Kowalski & T. J. Lasley II (Eds.), *Handbook of data-based decision making in education* (pp. 191–206). New York, NY: Routledge.

Datnow, A., & Park, V. (2010, May). *Practice meets theory of action: Teachers' experiences with data use.* Paper presented at the annual meeting of the American Educational Research Association, Denver, CO.

Datnow, A., & Park, V. (2014). *Data-driven leadership.* San Francisco, CA: Jossey-Bass.

Datnow, A., Park, V., & Wohlstetter, P. (2007). *Achieving with data: How high-performing school systems use data to improve instruction for elementary students.* Los Angeles: University of Southern California, Center on Educational Governance.

DiCerbo, K. E., & Behrens, J. T. (2014). *Impacts of the digital ocean.* London: Pearson.

Dieterle, E. (2014, May). *Discussion on learning analytics.* Paper presented at a presidential symposium at the annual meeting of the American Educational Research Association, Philadelphia, PA.

Duncan, A. (2009a, March). Federal leadership to support state longitudinal data systems. In *Leveraging the Power of Data to Improve Education.* Panel discussion at the Data Quality Campaign Conference, Washington, DC.

Duncan, A. (2009b, June). *Robust data gives us the roadmap to reform.* Keynote speech presented at the Fourth Annual IES Research Conference, Washington, DC. Retrieved from www.ed.gov/news/speeches/robust-data-gives-us-roadmap-reform

Duncan, A. (2009c, October). *Teacher preparation: Reforming the uncertain profession.* Address presented at Teachers College, Columbia University, New York, NY. Retrieved from www.ed.gov/news/speeches/teacher-preparation-reforming-uncertain-profession

Duncan, A. (2009d, May 20). *Testimony before the House Education and Labor Committee.* Retrieved from www.ed.gov/print/news/speeches/2009/05/05202009.html

Duncan, A. (2010a, June). *Education research: Charting the course for reform.* Opening remarks presented at the Institute of Education Sciences Research Conference, Washington, DC. Retrieved from www.ed.gov/news/speeches/education-research-charting-course-reform-%E2%80%94-remarks-secretary-arne-duncan-institutes-education-research-conference

Duncan, A. (2010b, November). *Secretary Arne Duncan's remarks to National Council for Accreditation of Teacher Education.* Retrieved from www.ed.gov/news/speeches/secretary-arne-duncans-remarks-national-council-accreditation-teacher-education

Duncan, A. (2010c, July). *Unleashing the power of data for school reform.* Keynote address presented at the Educate with Data: 2010 NCES STATS-DC Data Conference, Bethesda, MD. Retrieved from www.ed.gov/news/speeches/unleashing-power-data-school-reform-secretary-arne-duncans-remarks-stats-dc-2010-data-conference

Duncan, A. (2011, July). *Working toward "wow": A vision for a new teaching profession.* Remarks presented to the National Board for Professional

Teaching Standards, Washington, DC. www.ed.gov/news/speeches/working-toward-wow-vision-new-teaching-profession

Duncan, A. (2012a, January). Remarks. In *Leading education into the information age: Improving student outcomes with data.* Panel discussion at the Data Quality Campaign National Data Summit, Washington, DC. Retrieved from http://www.ed.gov/news/speeches/working-toward-wow-vision-new-teaching-profession

Duncan, A. (2012b, March). *World-class teachers and school leaders.* Opening remarks presented at the International Summit on the Teaching Profession, New York, NY. Retrieved from http://www.ed.gov/news/speeches/world-class-teachers-and-school-leaders

Dunn, K. E., Airola, D. T., & Garrison, M. (2013). Concerns, knowledge, and efficacy: An application of the teacher change model to data driven decision-making professional development. *Creative Education, 4*(10), 673–682.

Dunn, K. E., Airola, D. T., Lo, W., & Garrison, M. (2013a). Becoming data-driven: Exploring teacher efficacy and concerns related to data-driven decision-making. *Journal of Experimental Education, 81,* 222– 241. Retrieved from dx.doi.org/1 0.1080/00220973.2012.699899

Dunn, K. E., Airola, D. T., Lo, W. J., & Garrison, M. (2013b). What teachers think about what they can do with data: Development and validation of the data driven decision-making efficacy and anxiety inventory. *Contemporary Educational Psychology, 38,* 87–98. Retrieved from dx.doi.org/10.1016/j.cedpsych.2012.11.002

Earl, L. M., & Katz, S. (2006). *Leading schools in a data-rich world.* Thousand Oaks, CA: Corwin Press.

Easton, J. Q. (2009, July). *Using data systems to drive school improvement.* Keynote address presented at the 2009 NCES STATS-DC Data Conference, Bethesda, MD.

Easton, J. Q. (2010, July). *Helping states and districts swim in an ocean of new data.* Keynote address presented at the Educate with Data: 2010 NCES STATS-DC Data Conference, Bethesda, MD.

Educational Testing Service (ETS). (2005). *School leaders licensure assessment.* Princeton, NJ: Author.

Educational Testing Service (ETS). (2015a). *National Observational Teacher Examination.* Retrieved from www.ets.org/note

Educational Testing Service (ETS). (2015b). *Praxis.* Retrieved from www.ets.org/praxis

edX. (2015). *Introduction to Data Wise: A collaborative process to improve learning & teaching.* Cambridge, MA: Harvard University. Retrieved from www.edx.org/course/introduction-data-wise-collaborative-harvardx-gse3x

Ewing Marion Kauffman Foundation. (2015). *EdWise.* Retrieved from www.kauffman.org/microsites/edwise

Feldman, J., & Tung, R. (2001). Using data-based inquiry and decision making to improve instruction. *ERS Spectrum, 19* (Summer), 10–19.

Fenstermacher, G. D. (1994). The knower and the known: The nature of knowledge in research on teaching. In L. Darling-Hammond (Ed.), *Review of research in education* (Vol. 20, pp. 3–56). Washington, DC: American Educational Research Association.

Fullan, M. (2000). The three stories of education reform. *Phi Delta Kappan, 81*(8), 581–584.

Gage, N. L. (1978). *The scientific basis of the art of teaching.* New York, NY: Teachers College Press.

Girod, G. R. (Ed.). (2002). *Connecting teaching and learning: A handbook for teacher educators on teacher work sample methodology.* Washington, DC: AACTE Publications.

Greenberg, J., McKee, A., & Walsh, K. (2013). *Teacher prep review: A review of the nation's teacher preparation programs.* Washington, DC: National Council on Teacher Quality.

Greenberg, J., Walsh, K., & McKee, A. (2015). *2014 teacher prep review: A review of the nation's teacher preparation programs* (Rev. ed.). Washington, DC: National Council on Teacher Quality.

Guidera, A. R. (2013, April). *Defining the work: Effective data use at the local level.* Opening remarks at Changing the ground game: Focus on people to improve data use at the local level, Arlington, VA.

Guidera, A. R. (2014, February). *Welcome and introductions to data literacy.* Opening remarks at Empowering teachers with data: Policies and practices to promote educator data literacy [Forum and webcast]. Washington, DC: Data Quality Campaign.

Gummer, E. S., & Champagne, A. (2004). Classroom assessment of opportunity to learn science through inquiry. In L. B. Flick & N. G. Lederman (Eds.), *Scientific inquiry and nature of science: Implications for teaching, learning and teacher education* (pp. 263–297). Dordrecht, Netherlands: Springer Netherlands.

Gummer, E. S., Cohen, J., Gates, C., & Fantz, T. (2010, April). *Drawing deeper understanding from student solutions: A data analysis framework.* Presentation at the annual conference of the National Council of Supervisors of Mathematics, San Diego, CA.

Gummer, E. S., & Mandinach, E. B. (2015). Building a conceptual framework for data literacy. *Teachers College Record, 117*(4), 1–22. Retrieved from www.tcrecord.org/PrintContent.asp?ContentID=17856

Gummer, E. S., & Shepardson, D. P. (2001a). Facilitating change in classroom assessment practice: Issues for professional development. In D. P. Shepardson (Ed.), *Assessment in science: A guide to professional development and classroom practice* (pp. 39–52). Dordrecht, Netherlands: Kluwer Academic.

Gummer, E. S., & Shepardson, D. P. (2001b). The NRC Standards as a tool in the professional development of science teachers' assessment practice. In D. P. Shepardson (Ed.), *Assessment in science: A guide to professional development and classroom practice* (pp. 53–66). Dordrecht, Netherlands: Kluwer Academic.

Hall, G. E., George, A. A., & Rutherford, W. L. (1979). *Measuring stages of concern about the innovation: A manual for use of the SoC questionnaire.* Austin, TX: University of Texas.

Hamilton, L., Halverson, R., Jackson, S., Mandinach, E., Supovitz, J., & Wayman, J. (2009). *Using student achievement data to support instructional decision making* (NCEE 2009-4067). *IES Practice Guide.* Washington, DC: U.S. Department of Education, Institute of Education Sciences, National Center for Education Evaluation and Regional Assistance. Retrieved from ies.ed.gov/ncee/wwc/PracticeGuide.aspx?sid=12

Hammerman, J. K., & Rubin, A. (2002). Visualizing a statistical world. *Hands On!, 25*(2), 1–7.

Hansen, D. T. (2001). Teaching as a moral activity. In V. Richardson (Ed.), *Handbook of research on teaching* (4th ed., pp. 826–858). Washington, DC: American Educational Research Association.

Harvard University, Center for Education Policy Research. (2015). *Strategic data project.* Retrieved from sdp.cepr.harvard.edu

Haycock, K. (2001, March). Closing the achievement gap. *Educational Leadership, 58*(6), 6–11. Retrieved from www.ascd.org/publications/educational-leadership/mar01/vol58/num06/Closing-the-Achievement-Gap.aspx

Heritage, M. (2010). *Formative assessment: Making it happen in the classroom.* Thousand Oaks, CA: Corwin.

Herman, J., & Gribbons, B. (2001). *Lessons learned in using data to support school inquiry and continuous improvement: Final report to the Stuart Foundation* (CSE Technical Report 535). Los Angeles, CA: UCLA Center for the Study of Evaluation.

Honey, M., Brunner, C., Light, D., Kim, C., McDermott, M., Heinze, C., . . .Mandinach, E. (2002). *Linking data and learning: The Grow Network study.* New York, NY: EDC/Center for Children and Technology.

Hupert, N., Heinze, J., Gunn, G., & Stewart, J. (2008). Using technology-assisted progress monitoring to drive improved student outcomes. In E. B. Mandinach & M. Honey (Eds.), *Data-driven school improvement: Linking data and learning* (pp. 130–150). New York, NY: Teachers College Press.

Institute of Education Sciences. (2011). *Draft statement of work: Regional Educational Laboratories 2011–2016.* Washington, DC: Author.

Interstate Teacher Assessment and Support Consortium. (2011). *InTASC model core teaching standards: A resource for state dialogue.* Washington, DC: Council of Chief State School Officers.

Interstate Teacher Assessment and Support Consortium. (2013a). *InTASC model core teaching standards and learning progressions for teachers 1.0.* Washington, DC: Council of Chief State School Officers.

Interstate Teacher Assessment and Support Consortium. (2013b). *InTASC model core teaching standards: A resource for state dialogue.* Washington, DC: Council of Chief State School Officers.

Jennings, J. (2002). *New leadership for new standards.* Washington, DC: Center on Education Policy. Retrieved from www.cep-dc.org/publications/index.cfm?selectedYear=2002

Johnson, J. H. (1996). *Data-driven school improvement.* OSSC Bulletin Series. Eugene, OR: Oregon School Study Council.

Kearns, D. T., & Harvey, J. (2000). *A legacy of learning.* Washington, DC: Brookings Institution Press.

Kerr, K. A., Marsh, J. A., Ikemoto, G. S., Darilek, H., & Barney, H. (2006). Strategies to promote data use for instructional improvement: Actions, outcomes, and lessons from three urban districts. *American Journal of Education, 112,* 496–520.

Knapp, M. S., Copland, M. A, & Swinnerton, J. A. (2007). Understanding the promise and dynamics of data-informed leadership. In P. A. Moss (Ed.), *Evidence and decision making: 106th yearbook of the National Society for the Study of Education: Part I* (pp. 74–104). Malden, MA: Blackwell Publishing.

Knapp, M. S., Swinnerton, J. A., Copland, M. A., & Monpas-Huber, J. (2006). *Data-informed leadership in education.* Seattle: University of Washington, Center for the Study of Teaching and Policy.

Konstantopoulos, S., Miller, S., & van der Ploeg, A. (2013). The impact of Indiana's system of benchmark assessments on mathematics achievement. *Educational Evaluation and Policy Analysis, 35*(4), 481–499.

Kowalski, P. (2013, June). *Improving educator data literacy.* Paper presented at the annual conference of the National Association of State Directors of Teacher Education and Certification (NASDTEC), Austin, TX.

Kronholz, J. (2012, Fall). A new type of ed school: Linking candidate success to student success. *Education Next,12*(4), 1–8.

Lachat, M. A., & Smith, S. (2005). Practices that support data use in urban high schools. *Journal of Education for Students Placed at Risk, 10*(3), 333–349.

Leithwood, K., Louis, K. S., Anderson, S., & Wahlstrom, K. (2007). *Review of research: How leadership influences student learning.* Minneapolis: University of Minnesota, Center for Applied Research and Educational Improvement.

Lewis, M. (2004). *Moneyball: The art of winning an unfair game.* New York, NY: W. W. Norton.

Light, D., Wexler, D., & Heinze, J. (2004, April). *How practitioners interpret and link data to instruction: Research findings on New York City Schools' implementation of the Grow Network.* Paper presented at the annual meeting of the American Educational Research Association, San Diego, CA.

Long, L., Rivas, L., Light, D., & Mandinach, E. B. (2008). The evolution of a homegrown data warehouse: TUSDStats. In E. B. Mandinach & M. Honey (Eds.), *Data-driven school improvement: Linking data and learning* (pp. 209–232). New York, NY: Teachers College Press.

Love, N. (2004, Fall). Taking data to new depths. *Journal of Staff Development, 25*(4), 22–26.

Love, N., Stiles, K. E., Mundry, S., & DiRanna, K. (2008). *A data coach's guide to improving learning for all students: Unleashing the power of collaborative inquiry.* Thousand Oaks, CA: Corwin.

Mandinach, E. B. (2012). A perfect time for data use: Using data-driven decision making to inform practice. *Educational Psychologist, 47*(2), 71–85.

Mandinach, E. B. (2013, June). *Data literacy: Why it is important and why it is so challenging to attain.* Paper presented at the annual conference of the National Association of State Directors of Teacher Education and Certification (NASD-TEC), Austin, TX.

Mandinach, E. B., & Friedman, J. M. (2015, April). *Case studies of schools of education: What we can learn about improving data literacy among educators?* Paper presented at the annual meeting of the American Educational Research Association, Chicago, IL.

Mandinach, E. B., Friedman, J. M., Gummer, E. S. (2015). How can schools of education help to build educators' capacity to use data: A systemic view of the issue. *Teachers College Record, 117*(4), 1–50. Retrieved from www.tcrecord.org/PrintContent.asp?ContentID=17850

Mandinach, E. B., & Gummer, E. S. (2011). *The complexities of integrating data-driven decision making into professional preparation in schools of education: It's harder than you think.* Alexandria, VA, Portland, OR, and Washington, DC: CNA Education, Education Northwest, and WestEd.

Mandinach, E. B., & Gummer, E. S. (2012). *Navigating the landscape of data literacy: It IS complex.* Washington, DC: WestEd .

Mandinach, E. B., & Gummer, E. S. (2013a). A systemic view of implementing data literacy into educator preparation. *Educational Researcher, 42*(1), 30–37.

Mandinach, E. B., & Gummer, E. S. (2013b). Defining data literacy: A report on a convening of experts. *Journal of Educational Research and Policy Studies, 13*(2), 6–28.

Mandinach, E. B., & Gummer, E. S. (2015, September). *Using data for programmatic continuous improvement and the preparation of data literacy for educators.* Workshop conducted at the annual meeting of the Council for the Accreditation of Educator Preparation (CAEP), Washington, DC.

Mandinach, E. B., & Honey, M. (Eds.). (2008). *Data-driven school improvement: Linking data and learning.* New York, NY: Teachers College Press.

Mandinach, E. B., Honey, M., Light, D., & Brunner, C. (2008). *A conceptual framework for data-driven decision making.* In E. B. Mandinach & M. Honey (Eds.), *Data-driven school improvement: Linking data and learning* (pp. 13–31). New York, NY: Teachers College Press.

Mandinach, E. B., Kahl, S., Parton, B. M., & Carson, R. M. (2014, July). *What's the difference between assessment literacy and data literacy?* [Webinar].Washington, DC: Data Quality Campaign.

Mandinach, E. B., Kowalski, P., Ashdown, J., & Orland, M. (2014, September*). Schools of education and data literacy.* Invited symposium at the Fall conference of the Council for the Accreditation of Educator Preparation (CAEP), Washington, DC.

Mandinach, E. B., Kowalski, P., Farley-Ripple, E., Atkins, R., & George, J. (2014, March). *Why data literacy for teachers is important.* Invited symposium at the Teaching & Learning 2014 Conference of the National Board for Professional Teaching Standards, Washington, DC.

Mandinach, E. B., Parton, B. M., Gummer, E. S., & Anderson, R. B. (2015). Ethical and appropriate data use requires data literacy. *Phi Delta Kappan*, 96(5), 25–28

Mandinach, E. B., Rivas, L., Light, D., & Heinze, C. (2006, April). *The impact of data-driven decision making tools on educational practice: A systems analysis of six school districts.* Paper presented at the annual meeting of the American Educational Research Association, San Francisco, CA.

Mandinach, E. B., & Robinson, S. (2014, February). The role of teacher preparation in data literacy. In *Empowering teachers with data: Policies and practices to promote educator data literacy* [Forum and webcast]. Washington, DC: Data Quality Campaign.

Marsh, J. A., Pane, J. F., & Hamilton, L. S. (2006). *Making sense of data-driven decision making in education.* Santa Monica, CA: RAND Education.

Mason, S. (2002). *Turning data into knowledge: Lessons from six Milwaukee public schools.* Madison, WI: Wisconsin Center for Education Research.

Means, B., Chen, E., DeBarger, A., & Padilla, C. (2011). *Teachers' ability to use data to inform instruction: Challenges and supports.* Washington, DC: U.S. Department of Education, Office of Planning, Evaluation, and Policy Development.

Means, B., Padilla, C., & Gallagher, L. (2010). *Use of education data at the local level: From accountability to instructional improvement.* Washington, DC: U.S. Department of Education, Office of Planning, Evaluation, and Policy Development. Retrieved from ejournals.bc.edu/ojs/index.php/jtla/article/view/1621PADI.

Mitchell, D., Lee, J., & Herman, J. (2000, October). *Computer software systems and using data to support school reform.* Paper presented at Wingspread Meeting, Technology's Role in Urban School Reform: Achieving Equity and Quality. Racine, WI: EDC Center for Children and Technology. Retreived from http://cct.edc.org/publications/wingspread-conference-technologys-role-urban-school-reform

National Board for Professional Teaching Standards (NBPTS). (2015). *National Board standards.* Retrieved from www.nbpts.org/national-board-standards

National Center for Education Statistics (NCES). (2015a). *Statewide longitudinal data systems grant program.* Washington, DC: U.S. Department of Education, Institute of Education Sciences, National Center for Education Statistics. Retrieved from nces.ed.gov/programs/slds

National Center for Education Statistics (NCES). (2015b). *Statewide longitudinal data systems grants program: Grantee states.* Washington, DC: U.S. Department of Education, Institute of Education Sciences, National Center for Education Statistics. Retrieved from nces.ed.gov/programs/slds/stateinfo.asp

National Council for Accreditation of Teacher Education (NCATE) Blue Ribbon Panel on Clinical Preparation and Partnerships for Improved Student Learning. (2010). *Transforming teacher education through clinical practice: A national strategy to prepare effective teachers.* Washington, DC: Author.

National Council on Teacher Quality. (2012). *What teacher preparation programs teach about K–12 assessment.* Washington, DC: Author.

National Forum on Education Statistics. (2010). *Forum guide to data ethics* (NCES—2010-801). Washington, DC: U.S. Department of Education, National Center for Education Statistics.

National Research Council. (1996). *National science education standards.* Washington, DC: National Academy Press.

Neild, R. C. (2013, February). *Putting data to good use: Applying state and district data to improvement in education.* Keynote speech presented at Launching Data Initiatives: The 26th Annual Management Information (MIS) Conference, Washington, DC.

Next Generation Science Standards Lead States. (2013). *Next generation science standards: For states, by states.* Washington, DC. National Academies Press.

North Carolina Department of Public Instruction. (2013). *Data literacy.* Retrieved from, http://ites.ncdpi.wikispaces.net/Data+Literacy.

Olsen, L. (2003, May 21). Study relates cautionary tale of missing data. *Education Week, 22*(37), 12.

Peck, C. A., & McDonald, M. A. (2014). What is the culture of evidence? How do you get one? And . . . should you want one? *Teachers College Record, 116*(3). Retrieved from www.tcrecord.org/library/Abstract.asp?ContentId=17359

Privacy and school data. (2015, February). *Phi Delta Kappan, 96*(5).

Robson, D. (2015, August 14). Considered a data dinosaur, tennis tries an analytic approach. *New York Times,* B8. mobile.nytimes.com/2015/08/14/sports/tennis/a-data-dinosaur-tennis-tries-an-analytic-approach.html?emc=edit_th_20150814&nl=todaysheadlines&nlid=1524904&_r=0&referrer=

Rose, L. W. (2006). *Middle Start schools striving for excellence: Steadily improving high-poverty schools in the Mid South Delta.* New York, NY: Academy for Educational Development.

Rosselli, H., Girod, M., & Brodsky, M. (2011). *Connecting teaching and learning: History, evolution, and case studies of teacher work sample methodology.* Lanham, MD: Rowman & Littlefield.

Schafer, W. D., & Lissitz, R. W. (1987). Measurement training for school personnel: Recommendations and reality. *Journal of Teacher Education, 38*(3), 57–63.

Schmoker, M. J. (1999). *Results: The key to continuous improvement.* Alexandria, VA: Association for Supervision and Curriculum Development.

Schmoker, M. J., & Wilson, R. B. (1995). Results: The key to renewal. *Educational Leadership, 51*(1), 64–65.

Senge, P. M. (1990). *The fifth discipline: The art and practice of the learning organization.* New York, NY: Doubleday.

Senge, P. M., Cambron-McCabe, N., Lucas, T., Smith, B., Dutton, J., & Kleiner, A. (2000). *Schools that learn.* New York, NY: Doubleday.

Shaffer, D. W., Hatfield, D., Svarovsky, G. N., Nash, P., Nulty, A., Bagley, E., . . . Mislevy, R. J. (2007). Epistemic network analysis: A prototype for 21st century assessment of learning. *The International Journal of Learning and Media, 1*(2), 33–53.

Shulman, L. S. (1986). Those who understand: Knowledge growth in teaching. *Educational Researcher, 15*(2), 4–14.

Shulman, L. S. (1987). Knowledge and teaching: Foundations of the new reform. *Harvard Educational Review, 57*(1), 1–22.

Shulman, L. S. (2015). PCK: Its genesis and its exodus. In A. Berry, P. Friedrichsen, & J. Loughran (Eds.), *Re-examining pedagogical content knowledge in science education* (pp. 3–13). New York, NY: Routledge.

Stanford Center for Assessment, Learning and Equity (SCALE). (2013). *2013 edTPA field test: Summary report.* Stanford, CA: Author.

Stanford Center for Assessment, Learning and Equity (SCALE). (2014). *edTPA.* Retrieved from scale.stanford.edu/teaching/edtpa

Statewide Longitudinal Data Systems Grants Program State Support Team. (2015). *SLDS data use standards: Knowledge, skills, and professional behaviors for effective data use, Version 2.* Washington, DC: U. S. Department of Education, National Center for Education Statistics.

Stiggins, R. J. (2002). Assessment crisis: The absence of assessment for learning. *Phi Delta Kappan, 83*(10), 758–765.

Stiggins, R., & Conklin, N. F. (1992). *In teachers' hands: Investigating the practices of classroom assessment.* Albany, NY: State University of New York Press.

Sykes, G., & Wilson, S. (2015). *How teachers teach: A framework for teaching.* Princeton, NJ: Educational Testing Service.

Teacher Preparation Issues. 79 Fed. Reg. 71820 (proposed Dec. 3, 2014) (to be codified at 34 C.F.R. pts. 612 & 686).

TeachingWorks. (2015a). *High-leverage practices.* Ann Arbor, MI: University of Michigan, Teaching Works. Retrieved from www.teachingworks.org/work-of-teaching/high-leverage-practices

TeachingWorks. (2015b). *Measures of high-leverage practices.* Ann Arbor: University of Michigan, TeachingWorks. Retrieved from www.teachingworks.org/research-data/current-projects/measures-of-hlps

Thorpe, R. (2014). Residency: Can it transform teaching the way it did medicine? *Phi Delta Kappan, 96*(1), 36–40.

U.S. Department of Education. (2012). *Applications for new awards; Comprehensive centers program.* Washington, DC: Author.

U.S. Department of Education. (2014, November 25). *U. S. Department of Education proposes plan to strengthen teacher preparation: New rules build on reforms and innovation efforts to ensure educators are classroom-ready* [Press release]. Retrieved from www.ed.gov/news/press-releases/us-department-education-proposes-plan-strengthen-teacher-preparation

U.S. Department of Education. (2015). *The EDFacts initiative.* Retrieved from www2.ed.gov/about/inits/ed/edfacts/index.html

Urban Teacher Residency United (UTRU). (2014). *Assessment and data literacy scope and sequence.* Chicago, IL: Author.

Using Data Solutions. (2014). *Using data for meaningful classroom change: An online course.* Retrieved from www.usingdata.terc.edu/workshops/online_courses.cfm

Virginia Board of Education. (2008). *Virginia standards for the professional practice of teachers*. Richmond, VA: Author.

Wayman, J. C. (2005). Involving teachers in data-driven decision-making: Using computer data systems to support teacher inquiry and reflection. *Journal of Education for Students Placed at Risk, 10*(3), 295–308.

Wayman, J. C. (2007). Student data systems for school improvement: The state of the field. In *TCEA Educational Technology Research Symposium: Vol. 1* (pp. 156–162). Lancaster, PA: ProActive Publications.

Wayman, J. C., Cho, V., & Johnston, M. T. (2007). *The data-informed district: A district-wide evaluation of data use in the Natrona County School District*. Austin, TX: The University of Texas.

Wayman, J. C., & Stringfield, S. (2006). Technology-supported involvement of entire faculties in examination of student data for instructional improvement. *American Journal of Education, 112*, 549–571.

WestEd. (2015). *Data for decisions*. Retrieved from datafordecisions.wested.org

White House, Press Office. (2014, April 25). *Fact Sheet: Taking action to improve teacher preparation* [Press release]. Retrieved from www.whitehouse.gov/the-press-office/2014/04/25/fact-sheet-taking-action-improve-teacher-preparation

Williams, B., & Hummelbrunner, R. (2011). *Systems concepts in action: A practitioner's toolkit*. Stanford, CA: Stanford University Press.

Wise, S. L., Lukin, L. E., & Roos, L. L. (1991). Teacher beliefs about training in testing and measurement. *Journal of Teacher Education, 42*(1), 37–42.

Wohlstetter, P., Datnow, A., & Park, V. (2008). Creating a system for data-driven decision-making: Applying the principal-agent-framework. *School Effectiveness and School Improvement, 19*(3), 239–259.

Worrell, F. C., Brabeck, M. M., Dwyer, C. A., Geisinger, K. F., Marx, R. W., Noell, G. H., & Pianta, R. C. (2014). *Assessing and evaluating teacher preparation programs*. Washington, DC: American Psychological Association.

Zalles, D. (2005). Designs for assessing foundational data literacy. In *On the cutting edge: Strong undergraduate geoscience teaching: Essays about observing and assessing student learning*. Retrieved from serc.carleton.edu/NAGTWorkshops/assess/essays.html

# Index

AACTE (American Association of Colleges for Teacher Education), 23, 35–36, 101, 102, 118

Administrators. *See* School administrators; School districts

AERA (American Educational Research Association), 24, 36

AFT (American Federation of Teachers), 26, 120

Aguerrebere, Joe, 23

Airola, D. T., 58, 59

Alliance for Excellent Education, 23–24

Alonzo, J., 59

American Association of Colleges for Teacher Education (AACTE), 23, 35–36, 101, 102, 118

American Association of School Administrators, 120

American Educational Research Association (AERA), 24, 36

American Federation of Teachers (AFT), 26, 120

American Psychological Association, 25

American Recovery and Reinvestment Act of 2009 (ARRA), 22

Anderson, R. B., 12, 50, 63

Anderson, S., 7

Anthes, K., 6

Arizona, 10, 29, 116

Armstrong, J., 6

ARRA (American Recovery and Reinvestment Act of 2009), 22

Arter, J. A., 50

Ashdown, J., 118

*Assessment and Data Literacy Scope and Sequence* (UTRU), 37

Assessment literacy, 24–25, 26, 28, 29, 34–37, 39, 43, 66, 73–74, 77, 86, 88, 90, 97, 104, 107

*Assessment Task,* 123–124

Atkins, R., 119

Attendance data, 34

Bagley, E., 56

Baker, R., 10, 129

Ball, Deborah, 31

Bandura, A., 58

Barney, H., 10

Behrens, J. T., 10, 129

Beliefs of teachers, 45–46, 57–64
  about data use, 60–61
  in collaboration, 62
  in continuous inquiry cycle for improvement, 61–62
  in data use to inform teaching, 60–61
  self-efficacy and, 59
  that all students can learn, 60
  in value of data to communicate to others, 63

Bell, B., 22

Bergan, J. R., 10

Bettesworth, L. R., 59

Bienkowski, M., 10, 129

Blended learning environments, 10

Blue Ribbon Panel (NCATE), 23, 101–102, 118

Borman, G. D., 12–13, 105

Boudett, K. P., 92

Breaux, G. A., 24

Bridgman, P. W., 38

Brodsky, M., 74

Brunner, C., 5, 11, 12, 14

Burnham, C. G., 10

Bush, George W., 19, 20

Business, data-driven decision making (DDDM) in, 2

CAEP (Council for the Accreditation of Educator Preparation), 23–26, 31, 101, 118
Callahan, S. M., 10
Cambron-McCabe, N., 95
Canada, B., 22
Carlson, D., 12–13, 105
Carson, R. M., 36, 106
CCSSO (Council of Chief State School Officers), 24–25, 26–28, 35, 102
Center for Data-Driven Reform in Education, 12–13
Certification of teachers, 28–30, 87, 99–100, 115–128
Champagne, A., 97
Chappuis, J., 50
Chappuis, S., 50
Chen, E., 10, 13, 111
Chepko, S., 24
Cibulka, Jim, 12, 23–24, 118
City, E. A., 92
Cohen, J., 97
Collaboration
    of collaborative working groups, 8–9, 13
    data teams and, 7–9, 13, 111–112
    of schools of education with districts, 70–71, 80, 100–101
    teacher belief in value of, 62
Common Core State Standards Initiative, 23, 32–33, 98
Communication
    teacher belief of value of data in, 63
    teacher dispositions around, 64
Comprehensive Centers (U.S. Department of Education), 22, 116–117
Conative framing of domain, 45–46, 57–58
Confidentiality issues, 12, 20, 33, 49–50, 56, 63–64, 89, 93, 112, 113
Confrey, J., 13
Conklin, N. F., 89
Content knowledge, 18

expanding beyond, 46–47, 57–64
integrating with data literacy, 44–46, 74–75, 78, 97, 98–99, 110, 125
interplay with pedagogical content knowledge, 125
Continuous improvement, in schools of education, 70
Continuous inquiry cycle, 61–62. See also Inquiry cycle
Copland, M. A., 6, 7, 40
Council for the Accreditation of Educator Preparation (CAEP), 23–26, 31, 101, 118
Council of Chief State School Officers (CCSSO), 24–25, 26–28, 35, 102
Course design, in schools of education, 71–72
Craddock, Ashley, 83
Critical thinking, about teaching, 61
Curriculum of schools of education, 66–76
    curricular components, 71–75, 125–127
    education in data use, 66
    institutional components, 67–71
    research in developing curricular components, 125–127
    residency versus traditional programs, 65–67
    stand-alone versus integrative approaches to data-driven decision making, 15–17, 67, 72–74, 77–78, 79, 81, 85–86, 88, 90–91, 93, 96–97, 104, 121–122, 126
    transportability of programmatic impact into practice, 76, 81

Darilek, H., 10
Data. See also Inquiry cycle
    defined, 14
    ethical use of, 12, 20, 33, 49–50, 56, 63–64, 89, 93, 112, 113
    importance of, 20–22
    teacher beliefs about use of, 58–59, 60–61
    value in in communication process, 63

*Data and Assessment Literacy in Schools of Education* (Breaux & Chepko), 24
Data coaches, 7–9
Data culture
    impact of enculturation of data use, 129–130
    nature of, 5–6
    in schools of education, 78–79
Data dashboards, 10
Data-driven decision making (DDDM), 1–18. *See also* Data literacy for teachers (DLFT); Schools of education
    actionable data in, 107–108, 115–128
    in business, 2
    caveats and controversies, 31–34
    in the classroom, 112–113
    data sources, 3–4
    defined, 14
    implementation components, 5–10
    learning how to use data, 10–12
    legislation concerning, 22
    in medicine, 2
    outside the classroom, 113–114
    policy landscape for, 19–22, 115–117
    privacy issues, 12, 20, 33, 49–50, 56, 63–64, 89, 93, 112, 113
    professional organization influence on, 23–25, 118–120
    research findings, 12–13, 58–59, 103
    school administrator, 1, 14, 52, 68, 76, 79, 85
    in sports, 3, 62
    stand-alone versus integrative approaches, 15–17, 67, 72–74, 77–78, 79, 81, 85–86, 88, 90–91, 93, 96–97, 104, 121–122, 126
    standards and, 25–28
    state licensure/certification of teachers and, 28–30, 87, 99–100, 115–128
    teacher attitudes and beliefs regarding data use, 45–46, 57–64, 98–99

    teacher awareness of, 114–115
    in teacher preparation. *See* Schools of education
    tools to support, 4, 9–10
Data-Driven Decision Making (DDDM) Knowledge Test, 58
Data For Decisions Initiative, 93
Data inquiry cycle. *See* Inquiry cycle
Data literacy for teachers (DLFT), 4, 94–108
    assessment literacy compared with, 24–25, 26, 28, 29, 34–37, 39, 43, 66, 73–74, 77, 86, 88, 90, 97, 104, 107
    caveats and controversies about data-driven decision making, 31–34
    changes needed to increase capacity for, 103–108
    components and elements of, 47–55
    data-oriented beliefs and dispositions, 45–46, 57–64
    Data Use for Teaching framework, 44–45, 48–49, 54, 55–56, 64, 74, 78, 109–110, 112
    defined, 11, 38–40
    emerging trends, 92–93
    ethics and responsibility in, 12, 63–64
    expanding beyond content and pedagogical knowledge, 46–47, 57–64
    expert panel input, 42–44
    foundations, 15–16
    funding issues, 22, 103
    goals, 15–16
    hammer/flashlight metaphor, 103–104, 108, 121, 130–131
    importance of, 1, 10–11
    initial domain analysis, 48–49
    inquiry cycle for, 45–46, 47–55
    integrating content and pedagogical knowledge with, 44–46, 74–75, 78, 97, 98–99, 110, 125
    invitation for dialogue on data use, 55–56
    knowledge and skills in, 30–31,

Data literacy for teachers (DLFT),
    *continued*
    39–47, 97–98, 102–103
  legislation issues, 22
  nature of, 14, 16–17
  need for research on, 104–106
  need for training, 11–12
  noncognitive aspects of teaching,
    45–46, 57–64
  operational definition, 38–40
  policy and, 19–22, 115–117
  privacy issues, 12, 20, 33, 49–50,
    56, 63–64, 89, 93, 112, 113
  professional development materials
    analysis, 40–42, 43
  professional organization influence
    on, 23–25, 118–120
  questions, 15–16
  school administrators and, 11–12,
    39–40, 91, 100–101, 106, 121,
    122–123, 129
  schools of education case studies,
    65–83
  stakeholders in providing, 95–103,
    115–128
  standards and, 25–28
  state licensure/certification issues,
    28–30, 87, 99–100, 115–117
  survey of data literacy in schools of
    education, 84–88
  systems approach to, 94–95
  teacher attitudes and beliefs
    regarding data use, 45–46, 57–64
  tests for, 30–31, 58–59, 97–98,
    102–103
Data literacy for teachers (DLTF)
  in the classroom, 112–113
  data culture and, 5–6, 78–79,
    129–130
  developing teacher focus on data,
    88–92
  impact on practice of educators,
    128–129
  nature of, 110–115
  outside the classroom, 113–114
Data Quality Campaign (DQC), 12,
    24, 30, 36, 99, 103–104, 106–107,
    116, 118, 123, 127

Data skills, types of, 15
Data teams, 111–112
  nature of, 7–9
  power of, 13
Data Use for Teaching framework,
    44–45, 48–49, 54, 55–56, 64, 74,
    78, 109–110, 112
Data warehouses, 9
Data Wise Project, 92, 101, 122
Datnow, A., 6, 7, 8
Dawson, E., 22
DDDM. *See* Data-driven decision
    making (DDDM)
DDDM Efficacy Assessment
    (3D-MEA), 58–59
DeBarger, A., 13, 111
Delaware, 116
DiCerbo, K. E., 10, 129
Dieterle, E., 10, 129
DiRanna, K., 5, 6, 7, 125
Dispositions of teachers, 45–46, 47–64
  around communication, 64
  to think critically about teaching,
    61
  to use data ethically, 12, 63–64
Distributed leadership, 7
District of Columbia, 29
Domain knowledge, 15–16
DQC (Data Quality Campaign), 12,
    24, 30, 36, 99, 103–104, 106–107,
    116, 118, 123, 127
Duesbery, L., 59
Duncan, Arne, 11, 12, 20–23, 65, 82,
    106
Dunn, K. E., 58, 59
Dutton, J., 95

Earl, L. M., 129–130
Easton, John Q., 5, 11, 20, 21, 40, 65,
    82
ED*Facts,* 19–20
edTPA, 30–31, 102–103, 123–124,
    130–131
Educational Testing Service (ETS),
    30–31, 102, 103, 130–131
*EdWise,* 98
edX, 92, 101, 122
*Empowering Teachers with Data*

(DQC), 24, 107
Ethics
    in data-driven decision making, 12,
        63–64
    privacy issues, 12, 20, 33, 49–50,
        56, 63–64, 89, 93, 112, 113
ETS (Educational Testing Service),
    30–31, 102
Ewing Marion Kauffman Foundation,
    10, 98
Expert panels, input on teacher data
    literacy, 42–44

Family context, 34
Family Educational Rights and Privacy
    Act (FERPA), 20, 50, 63
Fantz, T., 97
Farley-Ripple, E., 119
Fasca, C., 12
Feld, J. K., 10
Feldman, J., 6, 10
Fenstermacher, G. D., 58
FERPA (Family Educational Rights and
    Privacy Act), 20, 50, 63
Flashlight/hammer metaphor, 103–104,
    108, 121, 130–131
Formative assessment, 10, 32–33
Friedman, Jeremy M., 14, 28, 32, 43,
    46–47, 65, 74, 78, 83, 84, 99, 104,
    117, 120, 122, 123, 126
Fullan, M., 11

Gage, N. L., 60
Gallagher, L., 5, 8–9, 11, 13, 40,
    129–130
Garrison, M., 58, 59
Gates, C., 97
Gates Foundation, 95–96
George, A. A., 58
George, J., 119
Girod, G. R., 74
Girod, M., 74
Graduate Student Council, 24
Greenberg, J., 32, 85
Gribbons, B., 11, 12
Guidera, Aimee R., 103–104, 106, 130
Gummer, Edith S., 11, 12, 14, 23, 24,
    28, 32, 36, 39, 42–44, 46–47, 48,

50, 55–56, 63, 65, 74, 77, 78, 84,
    89, 95–96, 97, 99, 100, 104, 107,
    117, 118, 120, 123, 126
Gunn, G., 10

Hall, G. E., 58
Halverson, R., 5, 6, 8, 12, 14, 40, 123,
    129, 130
Hamilton, L., 5, 6, 8, 11, 12, 14, 40,
    123, 129, 130
Hammer/flashlight metaphor, 103–104,
    108, 121, 130–131
Hammerman, J. K., 13
Handheld devices, 10
Hansen, D. T., 57–58
Harvard University
    Center for Education Policy
        Research, 8
    Data Wise Project (edX), 92, 101,
        122
    Graduate School of Education, 92,
        101, 122
Harvey, J., 13
Hatfield, D., 56
Haycock, K., 11
Health Insurance Portability and
    Accountability Act (HIPAA), 50,
    63
Heinze, C., 12, 95
Heinze, J., 10, 12
Heritage, M., 10, 33
Herman, J., 10–11, 12
HIPAA (Health Insurance Portability
    and Accountability Act), 50, 63
Honey, M., 5, 11, 12, 14, 40
Hupert, N., 10

IES Practice Guide (Hamilton et al.), 5,
    6, 8, 12, 14, 40, 123, 129, 130
Ikemoto, G. S., 10
Inquiry cycle, 45–46, 47–55
    beliefs of teachers and, 59, 60
    continuous, teacher belief in, 61–62
    evaluating outcomes, 45, 48, 55
    identification of problematic issue,
        45, 47, 49–50
    keys to effective data use, 109–110
    nature of, 40–41, 45–46

Inquiry cycle, *continued*
  in schools of education, 72
  teacher belief in continuous, 61–62
  teacher dispositions around
    communication, 64
  transforming data into information,
    45, 47–48, 52–54
  transforming information into
    decisions, 45, 48, 54–55
  using data, 47, 48, 50–52
Inservice preparation. *See* Professional
  development
Institute of Education Sciences (IES)
  *Practice Guide*, 5, 6, 8, 12, 14, 40,
    123, 129, 130
  Regional Educational Laboratories,
    20–22, 117
InTASC (Interstate Teacher Assessment
  and Support Consortium), 23–24,
  26–29, 31, 57, 73, 75, 100, 102,
  117
Interactive whiteboards, 10
Interstate Teacher Assessment and
  Support Consortium (InTASC),
  23–24, 26–29, 31, 57, 73, 75, 100,
  102, 117
*Introduction to Data Wise* course, 92,
  101, 122

Jackson, S., 5, 6, 8, 12, 14, 40, 123,
  129, 130
Jennings, J., 12
Johnson, J. H., 11

Kahl, S., 36, 106
Katz, S., 129–130
Kearns, D. T., 13
Kentucky, 117
Kerr, K. A., 10
Kim, C., 12
Kleiner, A., 95
Knapp, M. S., 6, 7, 40
Konstantopoulos, S., 13, 105
Kowalski, P., 118, 119
Kronholz, J., 68

Lachat, M. A., 7

Leadership
  in data-driven decision making, 5, 7
  distributed versus central, 7
  in schools of education, 67–69, 79
Learning organization (Senge), 70, 78,
  95
Lee, J., 10–11
Leithwood, K., 7
Lewis, M., 3
Licensure of teachers, 28–30, 87, 99–
  100, 115–128
Light, D., 5, 8, 11, 12, 14, 95, 100, 123
Lissitz, R. W., 12
Local Education Agencies (LEAs),
  122–123
Long, L., 8, 100, 123
Louis, K. S., 7
Love, N., 5, 6, 7, 11, 125
Lo, W. J., 58, 59
Lucas, T., 95

Makar, K., 13
Mandinach, Ellen B., 5, 6, 8, 11, 12,
  14, 22–24, 28, 32, 36, 39, 40,
  42–44, 46–48, 50, 63, 65, 74, 77,
  78, 83, 84, 89, 95–96, 99, 100,
  104, 106, 107, 117–120, 122, 123,
  126, 129, 130
Marsh, J. A., 10, 11
Maryland, 116
Mason, S., 6, 9, 11
Massachusetts, 116
Massive Open Online Course (MOOC),
  92, 101, 122
McDermott, M., 12
McDonald, M. A., 122
McKee, A., 32, 85
Means, B., 5, 8–9, 11, 13, 40, 111,
  129–130
Medicine, data-driven decision making
  (DDDM) in, 2
Miller, S., 13, 105
Mislevy, R. J., 56
Mitchell, D., 10–11
Mobile devices, 10
*Model Core Teaching Standards and
  Learning Progressions for Teachers*

*1.0* (InTASC), 24, 26–29, 31, 57, 73, 75, 100, 102, 117
*Moneyball* (Lewis), 3
Monpas-Huber, J., 6
MOOC (Massive Open Online Course), 92, 101, 122
Mundry, S., 5, 6, 7, 125
Murnane, R. J., 92

NASDTEC (National Association of State Directors of Teacher Education and Certification), 23, 28, 119–120
Nash, P., 56
National Association of Elementary School Principals, 120
National Association of Middle School Principals, 120
National Association of School Boards of Education, 25
National Association of Secondary School Principals, 120
National Association of State Boards of Education, 120
National Association of State Directors of Teacher Education and Certification (NASDTEC), 23, 28, 119–120
National Board for Professional Teaching Standards (NBPTS), 23, 24, 75, 101, 105, 118–119
National Center for Education Statistics (NCES), 9, 19, 22, 82
National Center for Teacher Residencies, 77
National Council for Accreditation of Teacher Education (NCATE), 23, 101–102, 118
National Council of Teacher Quality (NCTQ), 32, 35, 85
National Education Association (NEA), 120
National Forum on Education Statistics, 12
National Governor's Association, 25
National Research Council, 11
NBPTS (National Board for Professional Teaching Standards), 23, 24, 75, 101, 105, 118–119
NCATE (National Council for Accreditation of Teacher Education), 23, 101–102, 118
NCES (National Center for Education Statistics), 9, 19, 22, 82
NCTQ (National Council of Teacher Quality), 32, 35, 85
NEA (National Education Association), 120
Neild, Ruth C., 20, 21, 82
*New York Post*, 39–40
*New York Times*, 3
Next Generation Science Standards (NGSS) Lead States, 98
North Carolina, 28
*NOTE Assessment Series* (Educational Testing Service), 31
Nulty, A., 56
Nunnaley, Diana, 18n1

Obama, Barack, 19, 20
Olsen, L., 12
Oregon, 58, 117
Orland, M., 118
*Our Responsibility, Our Promise* (CCSSO), 25, 35

Padilla, C., 5, 8–9, 11, 13, 40, 111, 129–130
Pane, J. F., 11
Parents, as stakeholders in providing data literacy for teachers, 123
Park, V., 6, 7, 8
Parton, B. M., 12, 36, 50, 63, 106
Peck, C. A., 122
Pedagogical content knowledge, 15–16, 18
    expanding beyond, 46–47, 57–64
    integrating with data literacy, 44–46, 74–75, 78, 97, 98–99, 110, 125
    interplay with content knowledge, 125
Personal digital assistants, 10
Personalized learning environments, 10

Personnel, in schools of education, 69, 79–80
*Phi Delta Kappan,* 12, 63
Policy context
  of data literacy for teachers (DLFT), 19–22, 115–117
  need for research on policy, 105–106
  policymakers as stakeholders in improving data literacy for teachers, 115–117
Practica, in schools of education, 75, 80
*Praxis Series* (Educational Testing Service), 30–31, 102, 103, 130–131
Preservice preparation. *See* Teacher preparation
Principals. *See* School administrators
Privacy issues, 12, 20, 33, 49–50, 56, 63–64, 89, 93, 112, 113
Professional development. *See also* Teacher preparation
  in data use, 58
  developing teacher focus on data, 91–92, 127–128
  emerging trends, 92–93
  at inservice level, 82, 91–92
  materials for teacher data literacy, 40–42, 43
  preservice preparation, 89–91
  stakeholders in improving data literacy for teachers, 95–103, 127–128
Professional organizations
  data literacy versus assessment literacy, 35–37
  influence on data-driven decision making, 23–25, 118–120
  as stakeholders in improving data literacy for teachers, 101–103, 118–120
  teacher preparation and, 23–25, 101–103, 118–120

Regional Educational Laboratories, 20–22, 117
Request for Funding (RFP) for the Statewide Longitudinal Data

Systems Grant Program, 115–117
Research
  on data-driven decision making, 12–13
  findings on teacher beliefs about data use, 58–59
  need for research on data literacy for teachers (DLFT), 104–106
  researchers as stakeholders in providing data literacy for teachers, 124–127
Rivas, L., 8, 12, 95, 100, 123
Robinson, M., 12–13, 24, 105
Robinson, Sharon, 23, 24, 36
Robson, D., 3
Rogers, Phil, 119
Rose, L. W., 6
Rosselli, H., 74
Rubin, A., 13
Rutherford, W. L., 58

Sagebiel, Micah, 83
SCALE (Stanford Center for Assessment, Learning and Equity), 30, 31, 102, 123
Schafer, W. D., 12
Schmoker, M. J., 10, 11
School administrators
  as data coaches, 7–9
  data-driven decision making, 1, 14, 52, 68, 76, 79, 85
  data literacy and, 11–12, 39–40, 91, 100–101, 106, 121, 122–123, 129
  high-stakes test data, 11–12, 102–103
  testing, 102
School districts
  collaboration with schools of education, 70–71, 80, 100–101
  as stakeholders in improving data literacy for teachers, 100–101, 122–123
*School Leaders Licensure Assessment,* 102
Schools of education, 65–108. *See also* Data-driven decision making (DDDM); Data literacy for

teachers (DLFT)
challenges of offering data literacy
    programs, 121
collaboration with school districts,
    70–71, 80, 100–101
curricular components of data use,
    71–75
data-related themes, 77–79
Data Use for Teaching framework,
    44–45, 48–49, 54, 55–56, 64, 74,
    78, 109–110, 112
developing teacher focus on data,
    88–92, 103, 104
emerging trends in educating for
    data literacy, 92–93
generalizability of data-related
    program components, 76–81
general themes, 79–80
implications of study for, 81–82
institutional components of data use,
    67–71
integrating data use in curricula,
    66–76, 90–91
overview of cases, 65–66
pedagogical implications of data use,
    109–110
possibilities of education in data use,
    66
residency versus traditional
    programs, 65–67
RP1 (case), 67–68, 69, 71–72, 73,
    74–75, 76, 77
RP2 (case), 67, 68, 69, 71, 72, 74,
    75, 76, 77, 78–79
RP3 (case), 67, 68, 69, 71, 72–73,
    75, 76, 77
scalability of findings, 81–82
as stakeholders in improving data
    literacy for teachers, 94–99, 101,
    120–122
stand-alone versus integrative
    approaches to data-driven decision
    making, 15–17, 67, 72–74, 77–78,
    79, 81, 85–86, 88, 90–91, 93,
    96–97, 104, 121–122, 126
survey of data literacy, 84–88
TP (case), 67, 68–71, 74, 75, 77, 78,

79–80, 81
transportability of programmatic
    impact into practice, 76, 81
Self-efficacy, 59
Senge, P. M., 70, 95
Shaffer, D. W., 56
Shaming, fear of, 33–34
Shepardson, D. P., 97
Shulman, L. S., 15, 16, 44, 46–47, 49,
    54, 97
SLDS (Statewide Longitudinal Data
    System) Grant Program, 9, 19–21,
    22, 74, 115–117, 125
Smith, B., 95
Smith, S., 7
Social learning theory, 58
Spencer Foundation, 95–96
Sports, data-driven decision making
    (DDDM) in, 3, 62
Staffing, in schools of education, 69,
    79–80
Stages of Concern Questionnaire
    (SoCQ), 58
Standards
    Common Core State Standards
        Initiative, 23, 32–33, 98
    data literacy for teachers (DLFT)
        and, 25–28
Stanford Center for Assessment,
    Learning and Equity (SCALE), 30,
    31, 102, 123
Statewide Longitudinal Data System
    (SLDS) Grant Program, 9, 19–21,
    22, 74, 115–117, 125
Steele, J. L., 92
Stewart, J., 10
Stiggins, R. J., 50, 89
Stiles, K. E., 5, 6, 7, 125
Student information systems, 9
Students
    as stakeholders in providing data
        literacy for teachers, 123
    support systems in schools of
        education, 75
Summative assessment, 32–33, 60–61
Supovitz, J., 5, 6, 8, 12, 14, 40, 123,
    129, 130

Support systems for students, in schools of education, 75

Survey of data literacy, 84–88
analysis of current data education practices, 87–88
courses to support data literacy in schools of education, 85
overview of survey responses, 85–87

Sustainability over time, in schools of education, 69–70

Svarovsky, G. N., 56

Swinnerton, J. A., 6, 7, 40

Sykes, G., 31

*Teacher Data Literacy* (Data Quality Campaign), 36

Teacher Practice Rubric, 72–73

Teacher preparation. *See also* Schools of education
data-driven decision making and, 23–25
data literacy in schools of education, 65–93
developing teacher focus on data, 88–92, 104
knowledge and skills for data literacy, 30–31, 39–47, 97–98
professional organizations and, 23–25, 101–103, 118–120
research on developmental needs of educators, 106
standards for, 25
state licensure/certification, 28–30, 87, 99–100, 115–117

Teacher Preparation Issues, 20, 21–22, 106

*Teachers College Record*, 48, 84

TeachingWorks, 31

Technology
MOOCs, 92, 101, 122
preservice preparation, 90
to support data-driven decision making, 4, 9–10, 92, 101, 122

TERC Initiative, 92, 122

Testing organizations
data literacy for school administrators, 102

data literacy for teachers (DLFT), 30–31, 58–59, 97–98, 102–103
as stakeholders in improving data literacy for teachers, 102–103, 123–124
testing movement and, 32–33, 34, 98, 102–103

Thorpe, Ronald, 24

Transportation data, 35

Tung, R., 6, 10

U.S. Department of Education, 9, 13, 20–22, 82, 106, 115–116
Comprehensive Centers, 22, 116–117
ED*Facts*, 19–20
as stakeholder in improving data literacy for teachers, 103

University of Arizona, 116

University of Michigan, 31

University of Virginia, 122

Urban Teacher Residency United (UTRU), 37, 72, 73, 77

*Using Data for Programmatic Continuous Improvement and the Preparation of Data Literacy for Educators* (Mandinach & Gummer), 24

Using Data Project/Using Data Solutions, 92, 101, 122

*Using Student Achievement Data to Support Instructional Decision Making* (Hamilton et al.), 5, 6, 8, 12, 14, 40, 123, 129, 130

UTRU (Urban Teacher Residency United), 37, 72, 73, 77

van der Ploeg, A., 13, 105

Virginia, 116–117, 122

Vision
for data use, 5–6
in schools of education, 79

Wahlstrom, K., 7

*Wall Street Journal*, 40

Walsh, K., 32, 85

Wayman, J., 5, 6, 8, 12, 14, 40, 123,

129, 130
WestEd, 93
Wexler, D., 12
*What's the Difference Between Assessment Literacy and Data Literacy?* (Data Quality Campaign), 36, 107
White House, 20, 21–22, 106

Whole-child perspective, 74, 80–81
Wilson, R. B., 10
Wilson, S., 31
Wohlstetter, P., 6
Wordle, 40, 41
Wyoming, 28, 29

Zillow, 33

# About the Authors

*Ellen B. Mandinach* is a senior research scientist and the director of the Data For Decisions Initiative at WestEd. Mandinach's work for more than a decade has focused on data-driven decision making at all levels of the education system. She has directed many projects that have examined how educators use data to inform their practice. Her work has appeared in numerous journals, including *Teachers College Record, Educational Researcher, Educational Psychologist*, and *Phi Delta Kappan*. Mandinach's books include: *Transforming Teaching and Learning Through Data-Driven Decision Making* (Corwin, 2012), *Data-Driven School Improvement: Linking Data and Learning* (Teachers College Press, 2008), *Remaking the Concept of Aptitude: Extending the Legacy of Richard E. Snow* (Lawrence Erlbaum Associates, 2002), and *Classroom Dynamics: Implementing a Technology-Based Learning Environment* (Lawrence Erlbaum Associates, 1994). She holds a Ph.D. from Stanford University in Educational Psychology.

*Edith S. Gummer* is the Education Research and Policy director for the Ewing Marion Kauffman Foundation where she oversees the development and implementation of the initiatives that focus on strengthening innovation and entrepreneurship in education. Prior to joining the Kauffman Foundation, Gummer was a program officer in the Division of Research and Learning in the Directorate of Education and Human Resources at the National Science Foundation. In that capacity, she was a program officer for the Discovery Research K–12 program that provided funding for the development, testing, and implementation of science, technology, engineering, and mathematics resources, models, and tools in preK–12 educational settings. Dr. Gummer's research has appeared in numerous journals including *Educational Researcher, Teachers College Record, Journal of Research in Science Teaching*, and *Journal of Engineering Education*. She holds a Ph.D. in Curriculum and Instruction from Purdue University.